# 5 STEPS TO A 5™

# AP Computer Science Principles

# 5 STEPS TO A 5™

# Computer Science Principles

**Julie Schacht Sway**

Mc
Graw
Hill
Education

New York  Chicago  San Francisco  Athens  London  Madrid
Mexico City  Milan  New Delhi  Singapore  Sydney  Toronto

1 2 3 4 5 6 7 8 9   LHS   23  22  21  20  19  18

ISBN      978-1-260-01999-5
MHID          1-260-01999-3

e-ISBN    978-1-260-02000-7
e-MHID        1-260-02000-2

Trademarks: McGraw-Hill Education, the McGraw-Hill Education logo, *5 Steps to a 5*, and related trade dress are trademarks or registered trademarks of McGraw-Hill Education and/or its affiliates in the United States and other countries and may not be used without written permission. All other trademarks are the property of their respective owners. McGraw-Hill Education is not associated with any product or vendor mentioned in this book.

*AP, Advanced Placement Program*, and *College Board* are registered trademarks of the College Board, which was not involved in the production of, and does not endorse, this product.

McGraw-Hill Education products are available at special quantity discounts to use as premiums and sales or for use in corporate training programs. To contact a representative, please visit the Contact Us pages at www.mhprofessional.com.

# CONTENTS

# PREFACE

Welcome to the future! Your future, that is. It will be filled with technology interacting with many areas of your life. You've taken this course to better understand many of the concepts that impact the use of technology. This knowledge will help you in any field you pursue, both for work and recreation.

This review book is designed to help you prepare for the AP Computer Science Principles Exam. Reviewing the concepts affords the opportunity to confirm those you are confident about and the time to dig into the ones you need to better understand before the exam. Let's get started!

# ABOUT THE AUTHOR

Julie Sway serves as the Technology Department Chair and Education Technology and Innovation Director at a 3K–12 independent school and serves as an AP reader for Computer Science Principles. During her career, she has worked for Coca-Cola USA, Coca-Cola Enterprises, Coca-Cola GesMBH in Vienna Austria, and Southwest Airlines as a software developer, project manager, auditor, and software quality assurance manager. While her experience in the business world provides insight into the skills and knowledge needed by introductory programmers, she is thankful she discovered the joy of teaching Computer Science to students and helping teachers integrate technology. Her experience in education includes instructional technologist, technology director, and classroom teacher. She is the founder of EdCamp Columbus, GA, and the Chattahoochee Valley Regional Technology Competition. She has presented at GISA and GaETC conferences on a variety of topics ranging from flipped classrooms to virtual fieldtrips. Julie is also a member of the Publicity committee for the GaETC conference and helps evaluate applications for the Innovation grants awarded by GaETC. Julie earned her BS in Computer Science from UNC-Chapel Hill and an MBA from Georgia State University. She has completed coursework toward a master's degree in Instructional Technology from St. Joseph's University.

Julie wants to thank her three children, Michael, Kathleen, and Elyse, for always providing inspiration and husband, Richard, for his support.

# INTRODUCTION TO THE FIVE-STEP PREPARATION PROGRAM

This book is organized as a five-step program to prepare you for success on the AP Computer Science Principles Exam. These steps are designed to provide you with the skills and strategies vital to the exam and the practice that can lead you to that perfect 5. Here are the five steps.

## Step 1: Set Up Your Study Program

In this step you'll get an overview of the AP Computer Science Principles Exam and gain an understanding of the format of the exam, the topics covered, and the approximate percentage of the exam that will test knowledge of each topic. You will also find advice to help you set up your test-preparation program. Three specific options are discussed:

- Full school year: September through May

- One semester: January through May

- Six weeks: Basic training for the exam

## Step 2: Determine Your Test Readiness

In this step you'll take a diagnostic exam. This test should give you an idea of how well prepared you are to take the real exam. It will also identify the content and skills you most need to review and practice. The multiple-choice questions on the diagnostic test are similar to those on the real AP Computer Science Principles Exam, so time yourself and discover what taking the test will be like.

## Step 3: Develop Strategies for Success

In this step you will learn strategies that will help you do your best on both the multiple-choice exam and the performance tasks. Learn how to attack the multiple-choice test and the Explore and Create performance tasks in the most effective and efficient way possible. Some of these tips are based upon an understanding of how the questions are designed, others have been gleaned through experience helping students prepare for the exam. and still others are based on experience grading the performance tasks.

# Step 4: Review the Knowledge You Need to Score High

In this step you will review the material you need to know for the test. The chapters are organized around the "big ideas" which form the backbone of the AP Computer Science Principles course and exam. Here you'll find:

- A comprehensive review of the concepts you'll need to know for the AP Computer Science Principles exam

- Key terms, listed at the beginning of each chapter, that you need be able to understand and be able to use

- Practice multiple-choice questions for each of the concepts tested on the exam

# Step 5: Build Your Test-Taking Confidence

In this final step you will complete your preparation by testing yourself on practice exams. This book provides you with two complete exams, answers, and explanations. Be aware that these practice Exams are *not* reproduced questions from actual AP Computer Science Principles Exams, but they mirror both the material tested by AP and the way in which it is tested. Use the exams to practice pacing yourself and build your confidence. You're now ready for the test!

# Introduction to the Graphics Used in This Book

To emphasize particular skills and strategies, we use several icons throughout this book. An icon in the margin will alert you that you should pay particular attention to the accompanying text. We use three icons:

This icon points out a very important concept that you should not pass over.

This icon calls your attention to a strategy that you may want to try.

This icon indicates a useful tip.

STEP 1

# Set Up Your Study Program

# CHAPTER 1

# What You Need to Know About the AP Computer Science Principles Assessment

**IN THIS CHAPTER**

**Summary:** This chapter provides basic information on the AP Computer Science Principles assessment. You will learn about the exam, the topics covered, and the types of questions asked. You will also learn about the in-class performance tasks (40% of your final AP score), which must be completed and submitted to the College Board in April before you take the exam in May.

**Key Ideas**
- ✪ The multiple-choice exam, administered early in May, contains 74 questions and is two hours long.
- ✪ In addition to the multiple-choice exam, you must submit an Explore performance task and a Create performance task by the April deadline.
- ✪ Your score (on a scale of 1–5) is determined by your scores on the component parts:
  - ✪ 60% of your total score is based on the multiple-choice exam
  - ✪ 24% of your total score is based on the Create performance task
  - ✪ 16% of your total score is based on the Explore performance task
- ✪ Most colleges and universities award credit for earning a score of 4 or 5. Some award credit for a score of 3. A list of individual college policies can be found on the College Board site, and you should always check with the colleges and universities you are applying to for their current AP policy.

# The Basics

The AP Computer Science Principles exam was first offered in spring 2017. More than 45,000 students took the first multiple-choice exam and submitted their Explore and Create performance tasks. One key goal of this new course, according to the College Board, is to make computer science more inclusive and accessible to all students. This course is an introductory course, equivalent to a one-semester course in college.

### The Format

The AP Computer Science Principles assessment consists of a multiple-choice exam (60% of your score), a Create performance task (24% of your score), and an Explore performance task (16% of your score).

### The Multiple-Choice Exam

There are 74 questions on the multiple-choice exam: you'll have two hours to complete them. For the first 66 questions, select only the best answer. For the remaining eight questions, you must select two answers. This is clearly noted in each of the last eight questions. Unlike other AP exams there are no free-response questions.

> There is no penalty for wrong answers so do NOT leave any questions blank. As with any multiple-choice question, if you are not sure, try to eliminate one or more of the answers. Then either go ahead and mark your best guess (recommended) or skip a line on the answer sheet. You can mark questions in your test booklet that you want to come back to. Later questions may help trigger your memory to determine the correct response for a question you were not sure about.

### The Performance Tasks

The AP in-class performance tasks assess skills that cannot be measured in the multiple-choice exam. Prior to the exam, you must submit two projects (called "performance tasks"): an "Explore" performance task and a "Create" performance task. These two projects together account for 40% of your overall AP score.

The Explore performance task requires you to investigate a computing innovation, create a computational artifact relating to that innovation, and provide a written response to question prompts. You will have at least eight hours of class time to work on this.

The Create performance task requires you to develop a computer program, submit a video of the program running, and answer free-response questions about the program you created. You will have 12 hours of class time to work on this project.

Your AP teacher will give you handouts that contain instructions for these two projects. The handouts are also available on the College Board's website in a PDF publication called the *AP Computer Science Principles Assessment Overview and Performance Task Directions for Students*. You can find this publication at https://apcentral.collegeboard.org/pdf/ap-csp-student-task-directions.pdf?course=ap-computer-science-principles.

Download and print out this PDF for future reference. You will need to refer to it often. It contains instructions for the exam, including the performance tasks. It also contains a copy of the exam reference sheet that you'll be given when you take the multiple-choice exam.

### Your AP Score

The multiple-choice exam is graded automatically by a computer. The Create and Explore performance tasks are graded by college professors and high school AP teachers who are teaching the course. They are trained and each project is evaluated and reviewed to ensure projects are graded consistently and fairly.

In the end you will be given a score on your AP exam that ranges from 1–5. The following table shows the meanings of the scores:

| AP Score | Recommendation |
|---|---|
| 5 | Extremely well qualified |
| 4 | Well qualified |
| 3 | Qualified |
| 2 | Possibly qualified |
| 1 | No recommendation |

Most colleges and universities award one-semester course credit if you earn a score of 4 or 5. Some colleges award credit for a score of 3. You should check with the colleges and universities you are applying to for their current policy regarding this AP exam. The College Board website has a list of the AP policies of individual colleges and universities, but to be sure, check directly with the school.

Being awarded college credit while you are still in high school has its advantages. You may be able to skip an introductory course and jump right into the elective courses you want to take. If you earn enough AP credits, you may be able to graduate early. Even if you don't want to graduate early, earning AP credit will give you more flexibility, making it easier to obtain a double major or study abroad. Another benefit is that you'll probably save money by not having to pay college tuition for course credits you've earned in high school. Perhaps most important, doing well on AP exams will help you stand out in the college admissions process, showing colleges that you're serious about studying and that you're able to handle college-level courses.

# What's on the Exam?

The AP Computer Science Principles Exam and performance tasks are designed to test your proficiency with six computational thinking practices and the seven "big ideas" covered in the course content. In this AP course, you'll not only learn about technology, but also about how it affects our lives.

### The "Big Ideas"

Taking this course introduces you to a broad survey of technology-related topics. These include the seven "big ideas" the course covers:

1. Creativity
2. Abstraction
3. Data and Information
4. Algorithms
5. Programming
6. The Internet
7. Global Impact

Step 4 in this book, where you'll review the content you need to know, is organized around these "big ideas."

The following table shows the percentage of multiple-choice questions you can expect from each of the big ideas in the AP exam.

| | |
|---|---|
| Big Idea 1: Creativity | 0% (Creativity is assessed in the performance tasks.) |
| Big Idea 2: Abstraction | 19% |
| Big Idea 3: Data and Information | 18% |
| Big Idea 4: Algorithms | 20% |
| Big Idea 5: Programming | 20% |
| Big Idea 6: The Internet | 13% |
| Big Idea 7: Global Impact | 10% |

## Computational Thinking Practices

Computational thinking is a driving concept in this course. There are six computational thinking practices the course references. They are:

- Connecting computing
- Creating computational artifacts
- Abstracting
- Analyzing problems and artifacts
- Communicating
- Collaborating

More detailed information on what's covered in the AP course and exam is available on the College Board's website in the PDF publication, *Computer Science Principles Course and Exam Description*. You can find it by searching by the title or you can go to https://apcentral.collegeboard.org/pdf/ap-computer-science-principles-course-and-exam-description.pdf.

## Who Writes the Questions?

AP exam questions are designed and tested by a committee of college professors and high school AP teachers. The process of introducing a new course takes years, and once available, the questions continue to be evaluated. This committee is also responsible for determining the criteria and rubrics for the Create and Explore performance tasks.

---

**The AP Computer Science A Exam—How Is It Different?**
The AP Computer Science A Exam teaches programming concepts using the JAVA programming language. It focuses more on developing solid programming and problem-solving skills. Taking one course does not preclude taking the other. They can even be taken at the same time. See the College Board site for more information about the AP Computer Science A Exam.

---

# Taking the AP Exam

### How to Register

If you are taking AP Computer Science Principles at school, the school's AP coordinator will contact you and help you sign up. If you are not taking the class, you should contact the AP coordinator at your school or school district for assistance in registering. Home-schooled students should either contact the AP coordinator for their school district or their assigned school to register.

The fee to take an AP exam in 2018 was $94. Check the College Board website for the most up-to-date information on fees. You can get a refund of most of your fee if you end up not submitting your performance tasks and not taking the exam. You may be entitled to a reduced fee if you have significant financial need; check with the AP coordinator at your school for more information about eligibility for fee reductions.

### The Dates

You should plan to complete the AP Computer Science Principles performance tasks by mid-April. The projects for the performance tasks must be submitted via an online submission process by the end of April. Check with your AP teacher or the College Board website for the exact due date.

The AP Computer Science Principles multiple-choice exam is administered in May. The actual date varies each year. Your AP teacher can tell you the date and time. You may get this information at the College Board's website: https://apstudent.collegeboard.org/takingtheexam/ap-calendar.

### Test-Day Policies

On test day, you need to bring the following items:

- Several pencils and an eraser that doesn't leave smudges
- A school-issued or government-issued photo identification
- A watch so you can easily keep track of test time in case there is no clock in the testing room

Items you are NOT to bring into the test room include:

- Any electronic device that can access the Internet or communicate with others
- Any food or drink, including bottled water
- A smartwatch or any watch that beeps or has an alarm
- Cameras or photographic equipment
- Any music device, including ear buds

# CHAPTER 2

# Planning Your Time

**IN THIS CHAPTER**

**Summary:** Preparing for the exam is important. The right preparation plan for you depends on your study habits, your own strengths and weaknesses, and the amount of time you have to prepare for the test. This chapter will help you get off to a good start by developing a personalized plan to prepare for the multiple-choice exam and the performance tasks of the AP Computer Science Principles assessment.

### Key Ideas

✪ Do not wait until the last minute to begin preparing. Develop a study plan and stick with it.

✪ Your study plan should be tailored to your needs, your study habits, and the amount of time you have available.

✪ Prioritize your review based on your strengths and weaknesses. Take the diagnostic exam in the next chapter to identify the areas you most need to review and practice.

# Three Approaches to Preparing for the AP Computer Science Principles Assessment

It's up to you to decide how you want to use this book to study for the multiple-choice exam and prepare for the performance tasks. This book is designed for flexibility; you can work through it in order or skip around however you want. In fact, no two students who purchase this book will probably use it in exactly the same way.

The first step in developing your plan is to take the diagnostic test in the next chapter. This is a practice exam that closely mirrors the actual multiple-choice exam. By taking the diagnostic test, you'll find out exactly what the exam is like as well as what you are reasonably good at and what things you need to review. Identify your weaknesses and focus on these first.

## The School-Year Plan

If you are taking the AP Computer Science Principles course as a one-year class, and if you find the course difficult, a full school-year test preparation plan may be right for you. Following this plan will allow you to practice your skills and develop your confidence gradually. You can use the chapters in this book for extra practice and another explanation of the concepts as you cover the same material in your class. Starting your study plan for the exam at the beginning of the school year will allow you to get to all the practice exercises in the book and maximize your preparation for the exam.

If you choose the option of beginning early, you can still start by taking the diagnostic exam in the next chapter. This will show you exactly what the multiple-choice exam is like so you know what you are up against. You can also find out what you already know. For this plan (and for the semester review plan), you have time to take the diagnostic exam at the beginning and again later in the year to check your progress and understanding.

## The One-Semester Plan

Starting in the middle of the school year will give you plenty of time to review and prepare for the test. This is a good option if you have only limited time on a daily basis to devote to test preparation either because you need to prepare for other AP exams as well, or you're super-busy with extra curricular activities.

With the one-semester plan, you should start by taking the diagnostic test in the next chapter. This will give you an accurate idea of what the multiple-choice test is like. You'll get a sense of how hard the test will be for you, how much time you need to devote to practice, and which types of questions or tasks you most need to work on. You can skip around in this book, focusing on the chapters that deal with the things you most need to work on. Be sure to find time to take both practice exams at the end of this book. Take the final practice test a few days before you take the actual test.

## The Six-Week Plan

OK, maybe you procrastinated a bit too long. But, if you're doing well in your AP Computer Science Principles class, you don't need to worry too much. And whether you're doing well or not, you still have time to improve your score by reviewing weak areas and practicing taking the test.

Start by taking the diagnostic test in the next chapter to find out what the actual multiple-choice test will be like and to identify content areas you most need to review. You don't have time to do everything in this book, so prioritize based on your weaknesses. If you find the diagnostic test difficult, try to devote as much time as possible to the review chapters. Save time to take at least one practice test and preferably take both of them. Even if you do really well on the diagnostic test and don't need further content review, you should take the practice exams at the back of this book to practice pacing yourself within the time limits of the exam.

---

**The Practice Exams Are Your Friends**

The practice tests are probably the most important part of this book. Taking them will help you do all of the following:

- Give you practice with the types of questions on the AP Computer Science Principles multiple-choice exam
- Allow you to measure progress and identify areas you need to focus on in your test preparation
- Allow you to practice pacing yourself within the time limits imposed by the test.

Save the last practice test for a final check at the end of April or beginning of May. But don't wait until the night before the test to take the practice tests. Staying up and trying to do some last-minute cramming may be counterproductive.

---

# Planning for the Performance Tasks

If you are in a traditional classroom setting, your teacher will determine when you begin to work on the Explore and Create performance tasks and time will be provided in class. The Explore performance task requires 8 hours of class time to be provided to all students, and the Create performance task requires 12 hours of class time be provided. You may work more than the 8 and 12 hours of class time allocated on your own. But don't get bogged down and spend too much time on them; stay cognizant of the preparation time you will need for the multiple-choice section and other AP exams you have.

If your class is a year-long class, your teacher may do full or partial practice Explore and Create projects first. These will help you better learn how to research and prepare the computational artifacts, written responses, and program. If you are taking this course as a semester-long course, your teacher may opt for practice performance tasks on a smaller scale or ones performed by groups.

If you are working in an independent study environment or home-school setting, you should complete the Explore performance task by the end of February at the latest.

You should not begin the Create performance task until you have a good understanding of abstraction, algorithms, and programming. All three of these will be incorporated in your program and the written response. These are covered in the Big Ideas 2, 4, and 5. If you are working on your own, begin the Create performance task in mid-March at the latest. If you are new to programming, you may need the additional time to learn programming fundamentals, and it may take longer to implement the concepts into your code.

Remember that once you begin the actual Explore and Create performance tasks, you cannot get help on the content of your projects. Your teacher, or anyone else, is only allowed to answer questions related to the project task, timeline, components, and scoring in general and not about your specific project.

Once these are finished and submitted to the College Board, 40% of your AP score is set. You then only need to spend time preparing for the multiple-choice section on exam day.

# Calendar: The Three Plans Compared

| Month | School Calendar Year | Semester Plan | Six Week Plan |
|---|---|---|---|
| September | Diagnostic Exam | | |
| October | Big Idea 2 | | |
| November | Big Idea 3 | | |
| December | Big Idea 4 | | |
| January | Big Idea 5 | Diagnostic Exam<br>Big Ideas 2 and 3 | |
| February | Big Idea 6 | Big Ideas 4 and 5 | |
| March | Big Idea 7<br>Practice Exam 1 | Big Ideas 6 and 7<br>Practice Exam 1 | Diagnostic Exam<br>Review weak areas |
| April | Review concepts as needed<br>Submit performance tasks<br>Practice Exam 2 | Review concepts as needed<br>Submit performance tasks<br>Practice Exam 2 | Practice Exam 1<br>Review concepts as needed<br>Submit performance tasks<br>Practice Exam 2 |

# STEP 2

# Determine Your Test Readiness

CHAPTER 3  Take a Diagnostic Exam

# CHAPTER 3

# Take a Diagnostic Exam

## IN THIS CHAPTER

**Summary:** Taking the diagnostic exam will help you identify the areas that you need to review as well as give you an idea of what the questions on the actual multiple-choice exam will be like. After you've completed the test, use the evaluation tool at the end of this chapter to identify specifically what chapters you most need to review and adjust your study plan accordingly. This diagnostic exam includes questions from all of the "big ideas" covered in the AP Computer Science Principles course except creativity, which is not assessed in the multiple-choice exam but is a key component of the Explore and Create performance tasks.

### Key Ideas

✪ Taking the Diagnostic Exam will allow you to familiarize yourself with the AP Computer Science Principles Exam.
✪ Evaluate your performance on this test to identify your own strengths and weaknesses and then modify your study plan to prioritize the types of skills or areas of content you most need to work on.

# How to Take the Diagnostic Test

Take this diagnostic exam when you begin to review for the exam. It will help you determine what you already know and what you need to spend time reviewing. It will also give you an idea of the format of questions on the AP exam.

Take the diagnostic exam in a simulated testing environment. Be in a quiet location where you will not be disturbed. Use the answer sheet in this manual and a pencil to answer the multiple-choice questions. The AP Computer Science Principles Exam is still a pencil-and-paper exam!

Set a timer for two hours and try to pace yourself so you finish the exam. If you are not finished when the time is up, note how far you got, and then complete the rest of the exam. Answering all the questions will provide a better evaluation of what areas you need to review.

As you take the test, mark all the questions you were not sure about so you check the answer explanations for them as well as those you miss. But do not check an answer until you have finished all the questions and the two-hour testing period.

Test yourself in an exam-like setting. Take this diagnostic test and the practice exams at the end of this book in a place you won't be interrupted for two hours. Time yourself. If you use your cell phone to time yourself, make sure it's completely silenced in airplane mode so you won't be interrupted.

In the next section of this book, you'll find helpful strategies for attacking both the multiple-choice exam and the Explore and Create performance tasks. The strategies were developed to help you prepare in the most effective and efficient way. Then in Step 4, you'll begin the review of the concepts and skills tested. After taking this diagnostic exam, you will know which of these chapters you need to review the most.

# Diagnostic Test: AP Computer Science Principles

## Multiple-Choice Questions
### ANSWER SHEET

1 (A) (B) (C) (D)    26 (A) (B) (C) (D)    51 (A) (B) (C) (D)
2 (A) (B) (C) (D)    27 (A) (B) (C) (D)    52 (A) (B) (C) (D)
3 (A) (B) (C) (D)    28 (A) (B) (C) (D)    53 (A) (B) (C) (D)
4 (A) (B) (C) (D)    29 (A) (B) (C) (D)    54 (A) (B) (C) (D)
5 (A) (B) (C) (D)    30 (A) (B) (C) (D)    55 (A) (B) (C) (D)
6 (A) (B) (C) (D)    31 (A) (B) (C) (D)    56 (A) (B) (C) (D)
7 (A) (B) (C) (D)    32 (A) (B) (C) (D)    57 (A) (B) (C) (D)
8 (A) (B) (C) (D)    33 (A) (B) (C) (D)    58 (A) (B) (C) (D)
9 (A) (B) (C) (D)    34 (A) (B) (C) (D)    59 (A) (B) (C) (D)
10 (A) (B) (C) (D)   35 (A) (B) (C) (D)    60 (A) (B) (C) (D)
11 (A) (B) (C) (D)   36 (A) (B) (C) (D)    61 (A) (B) (C) (D)
12 (A) (B) (C) (D)   37 (A) (B) (C) (D)    62 (A) (B) (C) (D)
13 (A) (B) (C) (D)   38 (A) (B) (C) (D)    63 (A) (B) (C) (D)
14 (A) (B) (C) (D)   39 (A) (B) (C) (D)    64 (A) (B) (C) (D)
15 (A) (B) (C) (D)   40 (A) (B) (C) (D)    65 (A) (B) (C) (D)
16 (A) (B) (C) (D)   41 (A) (B) (C) (D)    66 (A) (B) (C) (D)
17 (A) (B) (C) (D)   42 (A) (B) (C) (D)    67 (A) (B) (C) (D)
18 (A) (B) (C) (D)   43 (A) (B) (C) (D)    68 (A) (B) (C) (D)
19 (A) (B) (C) (D)   44 (A) (B) (C) (D)    69 (A) (B) (C) (D)
20 (A) (B) (C) (D)   45 (A) (B) (C) (D)    70 (A) (B) (C) (D)
21 (A) (B) (C) (D)   46 (A) (B) (C) (D)    71 (A) (B) (C) (D)
22 (A) (B) (C) (D)   47 (A) (B) (C) (D)    72 (A) (B) (C) (D)
23 (A) (B) (C) (D)   48 (A) (B) (C) (D)    73 (A) (B) (C) (D)
24 (A) (B) (C) (D)   49 (A) (B) (C) (D)    74 (A) (B) (C) (D)
25 (A) (B) (C) (D)   50 (A) (B) (C) (D)

# Diagnostic Test: AP Computer Science Principles

## Multiple-Choice Questions

Time: 2 hours
Number of questions: 74
The multiple-choice questions represent 60% of your total score.

**Directions:** Choose the one best answer for each question. Some questions at the end of the test have more than one correct answer; for these, you will be instructed to choose two answer choices.

Tear out the answer sheet on the previous page and grid in your answers using a pencil.

---

**AP Computer Science Principles Exam Reference Sheet**

On the AP Computer Science Principles Exam, you will be given a reference sheet to use while you're taking the multiple-choice test. A copy of this seven-page reference sheet is included in the appendix of this book (reprinted by permission from the College Board).

To make taking this practice test like taking the actual exam, tear out the reference sheet so you can easily refer to it while taking the test. Save these reference pages since you'll need to use them when you take AP Computer Science Principles Practice Exams 1 and 2 at the end of this book.

1. How are procedures abstractions in computer science?
   (A) They are blocks of code that do something specific.
   (B) They represent the lowest level of code for the computer to run.
   (C) They use actual values to represent concepts.
   (D) They can be used without understanding or seeing the code used.

2. What do parameters used in a procedure provide?
   (A) A way to get values into the procedure making code more flexible
   (B) A way to return values calculated in the procedure back to the calling program
   (C) A way to call a procedure from within another procedure
   (D) A way to connect an API to the procedure

3. What happens when you "clean data"?
   (A) Corrupt data records are corrected or removed.
   (B) Incomplete data records are completed or removed.
   (C) Duplicate records are removed.
   (D) All of the above

4. What causes a problem to be classified as "intractable"?
   (A) The solution is too inefficient for large datasets.
   (B) There is not an algorithm that can solve it.
   (C) It is solved most efficiently with large datasets.
   (D) Multiple algorithms exist with different levels of efficiency.

5. What are statements, procedures, and libraries examples of?
   (A) Low-level machine code that the computer uses to run the code
   (B) Abstractions used in writing software because they can be used without knowing the details of how they work
   (C) Algorithms that provide suggestions on how to approach writing the code to solve a problem
   (D) Pseudocode that helps design a solution for coding challenges

6. What is an issue that organizations must handle when dealing with large datasets?
   (A) Ensuring enough staff are on hand to process the data
   (B) Ensuring the bandwidth can handle the processing of the data
   (C) Ensuring that people's private data is not exposed
   (D) Ensuring the system can scale down after the data are sent to the cloud

7. How does the Internet work with the different equipment in use?
   (A) The routers adjust for the different equipment manufacturers by sending data on the same equipment brands.
   (B) Specific companies are approved to make equipment for the Internet.
   (C) Vendors follow the protocols established to enable data to be sent and received across any equipment.
   (D) The server farms handle the data once the data reach the Regional ISP (Internet Service Provider).

8. What does *scalability* mean?
   (A) The ability to build additional functionality into the hardware
   (B) The ability to build additional functionality into the software
   (C) The ability to add more features to the hardware
   (D) The ability to add or remove resources as the size changes

9. Why do we have high-level programming languages?
   (A) To make it easier for people to write code
   (B) So code will compile faster increasing efficiency
   (C) To make code reusable to speed development time
   (D) To prevent errors in programs

10. How can an image of a house that is used in a program represent an abstraction?
    (A) When pressed, code will run to return your screen to the home page.
    (B) The program directions to drive to your house will be displayed on your device.
    (C) Data about the smart features of your house will be displayed.
    (D) All the above

GO ON TO THE NEXT PAGE

11. How do selection statements determine which section of code to execute?
    (A) Through the use of the Turing algorithm for analysis
    (B) Through random number generators
    (C) Through conditions that evaluate to true or false
    (D) Through variables initialized to execute these statements

12. How are list elements accessed individually?
    (A) The list name plus an integer index in brackets are used.
    (B) The list name is used along with the value the code needs to access.
    (C) The "access" command is used with the list name and length.
    (D) A FOR EACH loop is used with the list to find an individual value.

13. What do logical conditions always evaluate to?
    (A) A Boolean value
    (B) A value stored in a constant
    (C) A "string" text field
    (D) A real number

14. What is an example of a coding-related abstraction?
    (A) Using comments in your code
    (B) The CPU (Central Processing Unit)
    (C) Pressing a button on an app
    (D) A constant value

15. What is the process where algorithms are used with historical data to attempt to predict human needs or requests for information?
    (A) Data mining
    (B) Trend prediction
    (C) Social analysis
    (D) Machine learning

16. There are many programming languages. How do computers understand the different languages?
    (A) Testing takes care of this for computers by confirming the correctness of the code.
    (B) Debugging handles this for computers by confirming the validity of the code.
    (C) Compilers and interpreters translate the code to machine language for computers to read.
    (D) There is a special natural language tied in to all programming languages that all computers can read that is created behind the scenes using abstraction.

17. How is a logic gate an abstraction?
    (A) It adds the detail needed for each logic condition possible.
    (B) It is more specific than hardware components.
    (C) It represents any true and false condition.
    (D) It is an integrated system of physical components.

18. How do APIs simplify writing programs?
    (A) By providing step-by-step instructions on how to use the programming language
    (B) By importing the newly written software to the API for others to use
    (C) By providing documentation on how to code the needed functionality
    (D) By connecting pre-written and tested software to a new program

19. While algorithms can be analyzed mathematically, what information does the empirical testing process provide?
    (A) It provides best, worst, and average case information about the algorithm.
    (B) It provides the maximum size dataset the algorithm can handle.
    (C) It provides the validity of the algorithm.
    (D) It provides the clarity of the algorithm.

20. Why is there a need to find different algorithms for problems that already have a solution?
    (A) Different algorithms could use heuristics rather than precise values.
    (B) Different algorithms could be more efficient.
    (C) Different algorithms could use frequency analysis.
    (D) Different algorithms could provide intractability.

21. Algorithms can be written with a combination of what three statements?
    (A) Sequence / Selection / Iteration
    (B) Series / Procedural / Functional
    (C) Connection / Collection / Recursive
    (D) Selection / Sorting / Searching

22. What is the most common way computer viruses are spread?
    (A) By people clicking on an infected file
    (B) From pop-up ads
    (C) Through network worms
    (D) From random botnet attacks

GO ON TO THE NEXT PAGE

23. What does Moore's law indicate?
    (A) That the power of processors would double approximately every two years
    (B) That the size of computers would decrease by half every two years
    (C) That the price of computers would decrease by half every two years
    (D) That the cost of computer storage would decrease by half every two years

24. How does creating program components help with program development?
    (A) Individual components can be added without additional testing.
    (B) Adding the components incrementally to working code helps create program functionality that is correct.
    (C) Multiple people can write the components and still ensure compatibility.
    (D) The components can be combined at once to create the needed program functionality.

25. What is the name of the search method that divides the size of the dataset by two with each iteration of the search?
    (A) Bucket search
    (B) Merge Search
    (C) Linear Search
    (D) Binary Search

26. How does documentation help with maintaining programs?
    (A) It journals the history of program changes showing how the program first worked before changes.
    (B) If code is modified, the documentation can guide the programmer in testing to ensure the functionality is still correct.
    (C) It documents how to run the program in multiple languages for a global audience.
    (D) It is useful for training new employees on how to learn the programming language.

27. What is the purpose of the DNS (Domain Name System)?
    (A) To translate natural language website names to their IP address
    (B) To create a new IP address for a website each time it is requested
    (C) To position the packets in their correct order
    (D) To route the Internet request on the way to its destination

28. What could a binary number represent?
    (A) A number in decimal
    (B) A color
    (C) Text
    (D) All of the above

29. How can programmers avoid duplicating code?
    (A) Through the use of selection statements
    (B) Through the use of iteration to repeat needed code
    (C) Through sequential statements to process all data once
    (D) Through the use of efficient algorithms

30. What is a problem that no algorithm exists to solve all instances called?
    (A) Indeterminable problem
    (B) Undecidable problem
    (C) Infinite problem
    (D) Exponential problem

31. What must occur before patterns can be identified in data?
    (A) Computational tools must process the data in iterative ways.
    (B) Algorithms need to be written for the patterns.
    (C) Abstracting out the details in the data must occur.
    (D) The data must be encrypted.

32. Why should procedures be used?
    (A) They ease the workload on the processors.
    (B) They facilitate the storage of data on hard drives.
    (C) They make writing and maintaining programs easier through reuse of code.
    (D) They control the flow of input and output data.

33. How should large datasets be analyzed?
    (A) Using information filtering and search tools because they are efficient
    (B) Using frequency analysis tools so patterns stand out
    (C) Using exponential tools for faster analysis
    (D) Using linear tools to see patterns as they develop

GO ON TO THE NEXT PAGE

**34.** What can help with identifying and correcting program errors?
(A) Revisiting requirements
(B) Collaboration
(C) Clustering requirements and tests
(D) Consolidating testing

**35.** How can financial transactions safely occur on the Internet?
(A) Through the use of symmetric keys
(B) Through certificates issued by Certificate Authorities (CAs) that validate the keys used
(C) Through the use of double authentication methods
(D) Through the use of frequency analysis

**36.** What is the definition of *bandwidth*?
(A) The frequency that data can be transmitted across the Internet
(B) The speed that data can be sent through the Internet
(C) The amount of data that can be transmitted in a fixed amount of time
(D) The delay between the request and the receipt of information on the Internet

**37.** Which type of loop is most effective to iterate over a list?
(A) Continuous
(B) While
(C) FOR EACH
(D) Do

**38.** What is one way to help ensure the correctness of algorithms?
(A) By testing with small sets of expected data
(B) Through the reuse of existing correct algorithms to build new algorithms
(C) Through documenting the functionality of the algorithm
(D) Through the use of heuristic algorithms

**39.** How has the sharing of information globally with experts impacted the medical field?
(A) Diagnosis and consultations can be done by non-local experts.
(B) There's been an increase in the sales of hardware needed to create the Internet to enable the sharing of data.
(C) Privacy laws have prevented the sharing of patient data on the Internet. It can be discussed online after sending the data using a delivery service.
(D) Social media sharing has increased the general public's knowledge of disease outbreaks.

**40.** Why do we use hexadecimal, a base-16 number system that uses 0–9 and A–F?
(A) It runs more efficiently than decimal.
(B) Computers use hexadecimal.
(C) It is easier to debug program errors written with hexadecimal.
(D) It takes fewer characters to represent larger numbers.

**41.** Why is it important to write programs that are readable?
(A) They are easier to modify and debug through use of good names, procedures, and formatting.
(B) They run more efficiently.
(C) They effectively process all cases of input.
(D) They produce accurate results.

**42.** How is collaboration useful in analyzing datasets?
(A) The multiple viewpoints can provide several outcomes for the data.
(B) Applying differing experiences and skills provides better analysis and insight.
(C) The analysis can be divided among several people, speeding up the analysis.
(D) Having multiple leaders helps the group form alliances based on interests.

GO ON TO THE NEXT PAGE

43. When would lossless data compression be preferred over a lossy one?
    (A) When you need to get back to the original file
    (B) When you do not need to get back to the original file
    (C) When you need to display the file on mobile devices and websites
    (D) When you have limited space available on your computer

44. How does cryptography enable the Internet to process transactions securely?
    (A) The public key encryption model is easy to use to encrypt data but intractable to decrypt for large numbers.
    (B) Frequency analysis is used to disguise the use of common letters in encrypted messages keeping passwords secure.
    (C) Symmetric keys are used to encrypt and decrypt messages for speed in processing to avoid being intercepted.
    (D) Polynumeric alphabets are used to encrypt and decrypt messages to allow for use with different languages.

45. Why are the Boolean logic values used in computer science?
    (A) Because most programs need to process both numbers and text fields
    (B) Because they are used to test a program's results to ensure the output is correct
    (C) Because they evaluate to true or false, which matches binary values of 0 and 1
    (D) Because they are useful to determine if an instruction is running in memory

46. Given the importance of sharing insight and knowledge gained from processing data, how can this be effectively communicated?
    (A) Using summaries of the insights
    (B) Providing detailed examples of the data to prove accuracy
    (C) Using tables and diagrams of the findings
    (D) All of the above

47. Why are models and simulations useful abstractions?
    (A) They can test hypotheses without real-world constraints.
    (B) They can change multiple options at the same time, leading to new insights.
    (C) They can precisely test real-world events to identify the ultimate outcome.
    (D) They can confirm the cause of events.

48. Why is "big data" important to science and business?
    (A) The investment in the time and expense of processing big data is large so the expectation for critical findings is huge.
    (B) It can identify trends or solve problems that smaller datasets may not identify.
    (C) It is too large to process when time is short, so businesses cannot use it effectively to react quickly enough for product changes.
    (D) It is useful to generate new research possibilities, so it is only important to science.

49. What is an example of lower-level abstractions combining to make higher-level abstractions?
    (A) Dividing functionality into separate modules that are all part of one program
    (B) Writing pseudo-code to identify what the program needs to do
    (C) Creating help documentation so the user will know how to use the program
    (D) Using a flowchart to identify program decisions

50. How is the Internet scalable?
    (A) Through the ability for additional networks and routers to be added without impacting service
    (B) Through the ability to add longer public keys to keep data secure
    (C) Through the ability to add additional authentication for users
    (D) Through the ability to add additional latency to requests

GO ON TO THE NEXT PAGE

**51.** How can social media have a positive global impact?
- (A) By allowing people to post their views anonymously and safely
- (B) By allowing accounts of unverified events to spread quickly
- (C) By providing a way for those impacted by disasters to communicate that they are safe
- (D) By posting images or videos without a person's permission to make them famous

**52.** What does it mean if a program runs in less time than another?
- (A) It is efficient.
- (B) It is correct.
- (C) It has been verified.
- (D) It provides economies of scale in processing.

**53.** How do parameters provide abstraction?
- (A) They block invalid input values.
- (B) They return calculated values from the procedure to the calling program.
- (C) They allow software reuse for different values.
- (D) They provide the detail needed for an abstraction to function.

**54.** Tracing what your code is doing is an example of which one of the following terms?
- (A) Discovery
- (B) Debugging
- (C) Shadowing the code
- (D) Scaffolding

**55.** How can an organization begin the process of analyzing data?
- (A) By following an iterative development process
- (B) By establishing measurements the data should show
- (C) By developing hypotheses and questions to test
- (D) By checking to see if the data matches previously collected data

**56.** What is an example of "metadata"?
- (A) A line of code
- (B) A header in a document
- (C) Author of the document
- (D) Test data

**57.** Why should we use an iterative development approach?
- (A) Because each iteration improves or adds code to build a successful program
- (B) To meet the legal requirements for code to handle sensitive data
- (C) To be able to begin coding while remaining requirements are being defined
- (D) To minimize the amount of time needed for testing

**58.** Which statement describes a good variable name in a program?
- (A) Variable names should be short so there is less opportunity for a typo.
- (B) Variable names should be descriptive to help others understand their purpose.
- (C) Variable names should start with program name and then the variable name for ease of tracking.
- (D) Variable names should begin with a number starting with 1, followed by 2, and so on to know how many there are.

**59.** How is hardware an abstraction?
- (A) Hardware is very specific and is therefore not abstract.
- (B) It builds physical layers of increasing generality to process machine code.
- (C) Hardware provides a specific way to run generalized software.
- (D) It uses general information about how it works at the lowest level.

**60.** Compound expressions can be created using which of the following operators?
- (A) IS / IS NOT
- (B) NOT / NOR
- (C) IF / ONLY IF
- (D) AND / OR

**61.** What does it mean when we say the Internet is redundant?
- (A) Parts of it are unnecessary.
- (B) If a path is down, packets can be routed a different way.
- (C) It has a delay between the request and the response to the request.
- (D) If there is an error, a backup system is brought online to be used.

GO ON TO THE NEXT PAGE

62. What are packets when referring to the Internet?
    (A) The delay in time from when a request is sent and received
    (B) The individual sections of the IP address
    (C) Information to be sent over the Internet broken into same size groupings
    (D) The intermediate locations that send information to their destination

63. What type of software tools can organize and filter data?
    (A) Word processing tools
    (B) Spreadsheets and databases
    (C) Interactive tools
    (D) Input/output tools

64. Which two measures are used to determine the efficiency of an algorithm?
    (A) The time needed to compile and the size of the dataset
    (B) The time to run and the memory usage
    (C) The number of lines of code and the size of dataset
    (D) The number of procedures and the number of loops used

65. What describes the process of keeping common or similar features and functionality while removing details that are different?
    (A) An algorithm
    (B) Decomposition
    (C) Simulation
    (D) Abstraction

66. Why is there a need for more than one programming language?
    (A) Some programming languages are designed for specific uses and are best used in those situations.
    (B) Some programming languages cannot implement needed algorithms.
    (C) Some programming languages cannot be compiled and therefore cannot run efficiently.
    (D) There is no real need, just the preference of those who create new languages.

67. What is the job of a computer's processor?
    (A) To calibrate the hardware
    (B) To determine how much memory is needed for a program task
    (C) To maintain the connections of all the computer's components
    (D) To handle the instructions when a program is being executed

68. What is a benefit of combining algorithms?
    (A) It saves time.
    (B) It minimizes complexity.
    (C) It increases flexibility.
    (D) All the above

69. How can you use an image on your website that you found on the Internet?
    (A) You can use it copyright free.
    (B) You can use it after paying a fee for use or obtaining written permission unless the author provided a Creative Commons license allowing such use.
    (C) You can use it if you provide attribution to the owner.
    (D) You can use it only if you do not plan to make money from it.

70. What does OSI (Open Systems Interconnection) do?
    (A) It's the process for sharing Open Source software.
    (B) It shows the steps to include in an implementation to communicate over the Internet.
    (C) It's the model for connecting continents with regional ISPs with fiber.
    (D) It's the process for breaking data into packets and reassembling them.

71. Which of the following list of hardware abstractions goes from least to most abstract?
    (A) Circuit diagram, truth table, logic gate diagram
    (B) Truth table, circuit diagram, logic gate diagram
    (C) Logic gate diagram, circuit diagram, truth table
    (D) Truth table, logic gate diagram, circuit diagram

GO ON TO THE NEXT PAGE

72. How are algorithms and programs related?
    (A) They have a hierarchical relationship.
    (B) Programs implement algorithms.
    (C) Algorithms implement programs.
    (D) They can both be run on a computer.

73. What should people do to ensure online sources are credible?
    (A) Review the author, publisher, and sponsor credentials.
    (B) Check to see if the site has anything that has gone viral to ensure credibility.
    (C) Read the comments at the bottom of the article to see if they validate the article's claim.
    (D) See how active the author is on social media for reliability.

74. What is a benefit of collaboration when writing code?
    (A) Collaboration allows the work to be divided among independent programmers to create.
    (B) Collaboration makes it easier to document another person's code.
    (C) Collaboration makes it easier to find errors.
    (D) Collaboration produces an increase in user requirements that can be met with more team members.

**STOP. End of Exam**

## > Answers and Explanations

1. **D**—We do not need to know how a procedure works only that it does. The details are hidden or abstracted away inside the procedure's code.

2. **A**—Parameters allow a procedure to be more flexible by allowing different values from the program to be sent to the procedure. Code does not have to be re-written each time it needs to be used in the program.

3. **D**—Cleaning data refers to taking raw data and checking it for errors. These errors could be corrupt, incomplete, or duplicate data. Cleaning could include either correcting or removing the identified data, depending on the specifications for a particular dataset.

4. **A**—Intractable problems may have an algorithm that can solve some or a small number of values, but as the dataset grows large, the algorithm cannot be used due to a lack of resources, either memory or storage.

5. **B**—These are some of the abstractions that can be used in writing software.

6. **C**—Organizations handling large datasets must protect the data to ensure people's private information is not accidentally revealed.

7. **C**—Protocols are a set of rules for a variety of services on the Internet. Data will move across any brand of equipment as long as the protocols are followed.

8. **D**—Scalability means adding more resources, such as servers to store data, as the dataset grows and removing resources if the size decreases. These resources can be added and removed without impacting the current processing.

9. **A**—Text-based programming languages are usually high-level languages that are very natural-language based; pseudo-code is a combination of natural language and a programming language; and block coding uses high-level commands that can be dragged to the program. Each of these makes it much easier for people to code since they each use more natural language-type features.

10. **D**—Each of the events could occur when the house image is pressed, clicked, swiped, or called in some way depending on the software using it. Code is executed behind the scenes as a result of these actions, so the image is an abstraction.

11. **C**—The code with the selection statement is executed if the Boolean condition evaluates to be true. Additional code can be executed if the condition is false using the ELSE statement.

12. **A**—Each element in a list has an associated index position, starting at 1. To access an individual element, use the list name and the index position in brackets. For example songList[4] references the fourth element in this list.

13. **A**—Logical conditions are in a Boolean format, meaning each condition will always evaluate to either true or false.

14. **C**—Pressing a button on an app is an abstraction because we do not know or need to know the details of what happens behind the scenes once we press the button. Clicking the button initiates code for the feature a particular button represents.

15. **D**—Machine-learning algorithms learn from and make predictions based on data to improve the experience for those using it. One example is search algorithms. These often infer additional details of your search criteria, such as showing the Mustang car versus the mustang horse if your other search criteria include automobiles.

16. **C**—Most programming languages are written in a high-level language that resembles natural language, such as English. This high-level code is translated to machine language that computers can then "read" and process.

17. **C**—Logic gates are physical circuits that perform Boolean logic functions.

18. **D**—APIs provide pre-written, pre-tested program modules to be used by other programs greatly simplifying the process of writing a new program. This helps speed up writing and testing the code as well.

19. **A**—Empirical analysis involves implementing the algorithm through code and executing it to determine best case, worse case, average case, and error rates.

20. **B**—Different algorithms can be created to solve the same problem. These algorithms could provide new insights to the problem as well as be more efficient.

21. **A**—All algorithms can be written with a combination of sequential, selection, and iterative statements.
    • Sequential statements run one after the other.
    • Selection statements are run only if the criteria are met.
    • Iterative statements repeat while a condition is being met and stops when it becomes false.

22. **A**—Viruses must be spread via an infected file. These are transmitted in ways to get people to click on them, and email attachments are the most common way.

23. **A**—Moore's law indicates that the number of transistors that can fit on a circuit has doubled approximately every two years. This leads to faster processors.

24. **B**—Developing program components and testing them before combining them with other working, tested code helps create large correct programs.

25. **D**—A Binary search uses the "divide and conquer" method to halve (divide by 2) the size of the dataset, and continues to search the half of the dataset the number could still be in. This search is very efficient, and the dataset must be sorted for it to work.

26. **B**—By documenting what the program does, if code is changed, the programmer changing it can test to ensure the functionality is still correct.

27. **A**—The IP address is a number with sections that is much harder for humans to remember and use. The Domain Name is the natural language name for an IP location, such as a website. The DNS takes the website name and converts it to its IP address for processing.

28. **D**—The same binary number could represent a number, color, or text field. The program using the binary number knows how to interpret its meaning for each step in the program.

29. **B**—Iteration sets up conditions where code can be repeated either a specified number of times or until a condition is no longer met.

30. **B**—Undecidable problems do not have an algorithm that can solve all cases of them.

31. **A**—Computational tools process the data in iterative ways so patterns can begin to surface.

32. **C**—Procedures are blocks of code that can be reused making the program more readable and easier to maintain.

33. **A**—Efficient tools, such as information filtering and search tools, are needed to process these very large datasets.

34. **B**—Collaboration is the process of working with one or more individuals on an activity or task. It is an effective way to test and correct code. The collaborative efforts could occur in person or in a virtual format, such as editing a shared document stored in the cloud or a video-conference.

35. **B**—Certificate Authorities (CAs) issue digital certificates that allow others using a site to ensure the identity of that site is authentic.

36. **C**—Bandwidth measures how much data can be transmitted from a location to another in a given amount of time.

37. **C**—A FOR EACH loop will check each element in a list from start to end without having to specify each one individually.

38. **B**—This is the concept behind libraries and APIs. Prewritten and tested algorithms and code can be used by other programs needing the same functionality in their program. It saves time as well as helps ensure the new algorithms are correct.

39. **A**—With the increased ease of sharing and protecting information, doctors are now able to consult with other doctors located worldwide.

40. **D**—Hexadecimal can use fewer characters to represent larger numbers than binary. Hexadecimal needs 16 characters to represent numbers from 0–15. Since we run out of single digit numbers after 9, the letters A, B, C, D, E, and F are used for 10–15 in hexadecimal.

    | | |
    |---|---|
    | A = 10 | D = 13 |
    | B = 11 | E = 14 |
    | C = 12 | F = 15 |

41. **A**—Readability makes code easier to understand and therefore easier to debug, maintain, and enhance.

42. **B**—Having people with different perspectives and backgrounds helps identify new trends and potential solutions more easily than someone working alone or a homogeneous group.

43. **A**—Lossless data compression techniques enable the original, uncompressed file to be restored. Lossless techniques do not provide as much compression as a lossy technique, but always select this when you may need to restore the original file.

44. **A**—A good cryptographic model is easy to use in one direction, such as encrypting data, but very difficult to do in the other direction, the decryption of the data. This means that even if the information is intercepted, someone trying to exploit it may still not be able to identify the correct encryption key used.

45. **C**—Boolean logic can be used at a simple level or to build more complex conditions to represent needed functionality, but always evaluate to be true or false. This is useful in computer science where at its lowest level, machine code is made up of 0s and 1s.

46. **D**—There are many effective strategies for sharing the information gained. Choosing an appropriate level of detail and presentation method based on the audience is important to clearly communicate the findings.

47. **A**—While models are usually on a smaller scale than the real-world feature they represent, they can be used to simulate actual events to see the result of changes to variables. These can be run without actual constraints, such as emulating an eclipse without having to wait for an actual eclipse to occur to test the hypotheses.

48. **B**—Because of the sheer volume of data, both scientists and businesses have far more data to sift through to identify more insights than humans could possibly manage, making it useful to both.

49. **A**—Each module handles functionality independently but can be combined with other modules to create new functionality. For example, if a module adds a text field to a list, it can be added to functionality to create and maintain a contact list on a smartphone.

50. **A**—As the demand for Internet connections grows, new networks can be added along with additional routers as needed, without impacting existing service levels.

51. **C**—Social media, including blogs and Twitter, have helped spread information, both positive and negative. In a disaster situation, people often have their mobile device, and may be able to signal for help and communicate to family members that they are safe.

52. **A**—One algorithm is considered to be more efficient than another if it runs in less time for the same dataset. Efficiency may change as datasets get increasingly large. The more efficient algorithm will require less time and resources to successfully complete.

53. **C**—Parameter use enables a procedure to be more general, and therefore more abstract, by providing a way to get different values to the block of code.

54. **B**—One method of debugging involves following or tracing each line of code to determine what the program is doing versus what it should be doing based on current variable values.

55. **C**—Developing hypotheses and questions and testing these with the data helps gain insight.

56. **C**—*Metadata* means "data about data." The only option that provides information about the data versus being data is information about the author.

GO ON TO THE NEXT PAGE

57. **A**—The steps are:
    - Investigate and fully define the problem to be solved
    - Plan to fully understand the scope of the problem
    - Design to identify a solution to solve the problem
    - Create to code the solution
    - Test to evaluate the solution
    - Document to create "how to" documentation along with comments to clarify the code

58. **B**—Variable names should be descriptive and use "camel case" by capitalizing the second and additional words, when two or more words are used for the variable name. Example: shoeSize

59. **B**—It makes use of the transistors at increasing levels of abstraction in physical layers to process binary data.

60. **D**—Using the AND and OR operators create a compound expression. Both conditions for the AND must be true for the expression to be true, and at least one of the conditions needs to be true for an OR compound expression to be true.

61. **B**—Internet redundancy means that if a path is down, then the packets can be sent via an alternate route to reach their destination.

62. **C**—Packets are same size groupings of information to be sent over the Internet along different paths.

63. **B**—Technology tools such as spreadsheets and databases are designed to organize data and easily set up inquiries and reports to analyze the data.

64. **B**—The efficiency of an algorithm measures the runtime or memory requirements as the size of the dataset increases. Algorithms with logarithmic efficiency are most efficient, followed by linear, and then quadratic efficiency.

65. **D**—Abstractions remove differing details to create a more general and more flexible concept.

66. **A**—Most programming languages can implement an algorithm, but some were designed for specific uses, such as for scientific calculations, and are best used in those situations.

67. **D**—The computer's processor, or CPU, handles all the instructions for programs that are actively running.

68. **D**—All answers are correct. Combining algorithms saves time because you can reuse ones previously written and tested. Complexity is minimized because functionality is separated out into different modules, making it easier to identify unique functionality, and only coding it once. Flexibility is increased as different values can be passed to the algorithms so the same one can be used for many different values.

69. **B**—The Creative Commons licensing options allow creators to make their work available for view, and possibly for use by others, depending on the licensing option selected. Always note that artifacts on the Internet are not necessarily free. They are someone else's intellectual property. You may not use it without paying the licensing fee or obtaining written permission from the owner to use it, even in an educational project.

70. **B**—OSI is a model for how to communicate over the Internet. Those who create a new way to do this must include the OSI steps to work successfully.

71. **A**—Like many aspects of computer science, abstractions are represented as a hierarchy from least abstract on the bottom to most abstract. The circuit diagram is very specific. The truth table shows the same combinations but uses true and false to represent the outcomes. The logic gate diagram uses symbols for the functionality making it the most abstract.

72. **B**—Algorithms are identified first, and then programs are written to implement the algorithm's design.

73. **A**—In addition to finding information easily, technology tools can help determine the validity of the author.

74. **C**—Collaboration can help find and correct errors when developing and testing programs.

# Analyzing Your Performance on the Diagnostic Test

The exercise below will help you quickly and easily identify the chapters in Step 4 that you most need to review for the AP Computer Science Principles multiple-choice exam. Revise your study plan so that you prioritize the chapters with which you had the most difficulty.

Look at your answer sheet and mark all the questions you missed. Then shade in or mark an X in the boxes below that correspond to the question numbers that you missed. For what concepts did you miss the most questions?

Chapter 6: Abstraction

| 1 | 5 | 14 | 16 | 17 | 28 | 40 |
|---|---|----|----|----|----|----|
| 45 | 47 | 49 | 53 | 59 | 65 | 71 |

Chapter 7: Data and Information

| 3 | 6 | 8 | 31 | 33 | 34 | 42 |
|---|---|---|----|----|----|----|
| 43 | 46 | 48 | 55 | 56 | 63 | |

Chapter 8: Algorithms

| 4 | 9 | 11 | 19 | 20 | 21 | 25 |
|---|---|----|----|----|----|----|
| 30 | 38 | 41 | 52 | 64 | 66 | 68 |

Chapter 9: Programming

| 2 | 12 | 13 | 18 | 24 | 26 | 32 | 37 |
|---|----|----|----|----|----|----|----|
| 54 | 57 | 58 | 60 | 67 | 72 | 74 | |

Chapter 10: The Internet

| 7 | 22 | 27 | 35 | 36 |
|---|----|----|----|----|
| 44 | 50 | 61 | 62 | 70 |

Chapter 11: Global Impact

| 10 | 15 | 23 | 39 | 51 | 69 | 73 |
|----|----|----|----|----|----|----|

# STEP 3

# Develop Strategies for Success

CHAPTER **4** Strategies to Help You Do Your Best
on the Exam

# CHAPTER 4

# Strategies to Help You Do Your Best on the Exam

IN THIS CHAPTER

**Summary:** This chapter contains strategies and tips for answering the multiple-choice questions of the AP Computer Science Principles Exam. You'll also find strategies to approach and master the performance tasks. Understanding how to most effectively and efficiently take the test will help you get a higher score.

**Key Ideas**

✪ Practice pacing yourself on the multiple-choice exam. Don't get bogged down on questions you don't understand. Your goal is to get to the end of the exam so you get every point possible for the questions you know.

✪ If you don't know an answer on the multiple-choice exam, use the process to eliminate one or more answer choices and then guess. Don't leave any question blank.

✪ Planning, collaborating where allowed, and carefully editing your written responses to conform to the scoring rubric are keys to doing well on the performance tasks.

# Strategies and Tips for the Multiple-Choice Exam

It's safe to say that this will *not* be the first timed multiple-choice exam you've ever taken. You're familiar with how this works and have probably already developed your own style to approach this type of test. To get the highest score you are capable of, it's necessary that your method is as efficient and effective as possible. Look at the strategies below and make sure you're on the right track.

### Strategy #1: Pace Yourself

Many students approach the test with the lofty goal of getting every answer correct. But this approach will get you bogged down in the difficult questions where you are not sure of the answer. You'll end up not completing the test and missing questions you could easily have gotten right. Keep in mind that you can miss a number of multiple-choice questions and still get a 5. The best strategy in approaching the test is not to worry about missing some questions; instead try to make sure you get to every question for which you know the answer.

The AP Computer Science Principles Exam does *not* start out with easy questions and work its way up to the hard ones. Questions are randomly ordered so the questions that are easy for you are just as likely to be at the end as at the beginning of the test. Remember, you get the same number of points for getting an easy question right as a hard question. Don't bring down your score by not getting to all the questions for which you know the answer. If you don't know an answer, take a guess and move on. You need to get to the last question of the exam in order to maximize the number of questions you answer correctly.

Practice pacing yourself by taking the practice tests in this book and timing yourself. You have to answer 74 questions in two hours. So, you need to answer 37 questions per hour, or 18 to 19 every half hour. That's about a minute and a half per question. Keep track of your pace as you work. Ideally, you'll want to work a little faster so that at the end you have time to go back to questions you want to think more about (more about that in the next section).

The difficult questions are not the only ones that may slow you down. Don't spend time second-guessing a choice you made. This is usually a waste of valuable time. Trust your initial instincts and don't change an answer unless you are certain it needs changing.

### Strategy #2: Use the Process of Elimination and Guess

You're probably familiar with this strategy from all the timed multiple-choice exams you've taken. The correct answer is right in front of you. If you don't know which one it is, immediately start eliminating answer choices you're pretty sure are wrong. If you can eliminate even one choice as incorrect, your odds of getting the question right improve. If you can eliminate two wrong answer choices, you have a good chance of guessing correctly between the two remaining choices.

Even if you can't eliminate a single wrong answer choice, you should still guess. There is no penalty for guessing incorrectly so make sure an oval is filled in for every question.

Mark questions you want to come back to at the end if you have time. Perhaps another question will jog your memory or even offer a clue. You should try to work fast enough so that you have a little time at the end to do this. But be sure to mark the question in your test booklet, not on your answer sheet. Keep all unnecessary pencil marks off your answer sheet so that the computer that scores the test doesn't misread your marks.

Even if it's a question you want to come back to, fill in an answer choice. Don't leave it blank. You may not have time to come back. Also, marking an oval will reduce the chance that you'll mess up your answer sheet. Your worst nightmare is answering the questions correctly, but getting off a row in filling in the ovals.

The process of elimination is even more powerful when used for the eight final multiple-choice questions for which you'll need to select *two* correct answers. Fill in *two* ovals for each of these questions. If you can eliminate just two wrong answers, you'll get the question right. But, keep in mind that there's no partial credit; to get the question right, you'll need to have identified both correct answers.

## Helpful Tips for the Multiple-Choice Exam

### Reading the Question

- Read each question all the way through. Don't guess what the final question or instruction is. Note that the instruction to choose *two* answer choices is given at the end.
- Watch for words like *not, never, least, most,* and *always.* Be especially careful in selecting an answer when one of these negative words appears.
- Think of your answer before reading the choices. This can save you time and keep any distractors from making you second-guess your response.
- Read all the answer choices. Do NOT stop at the first choice you think is correct. There may be a better answer further down the choices.
- If the answer choices are not what you would expect, it's possible you misread or misunderstood the question. Read the question again and again until you understand what it is asking.

### Choosing an Answer

- Guess if you do not know the answer. There is no penalty for wrong answers.
- Mark questions you want to come back to if you have time at the end. Mark them in the question booklet, not the answer sheet, where any stray pencil mark may be misread by the computer.
- Do not change an answer unless you are certain. Trust your initial instincts.
- Do NOT change an answer because you see there are several answers of the same letter in a row! Don't worry if you seem to be marking a lot of one letter in your answer choices.

### Marking the Answer Sheet

- Fill in the bubbles on the answer sheet completely. But don't make other marks on your answer sheet.
- If you need to erase an answer, make sure it's completely erased so that the computer won't read that you filled in two ovals. Bring an eraser that won't leave smudges.
- Be sure you are filling in the answer for the correct question. Check each time you turn the page to be sure. There's nothing worse than getting the question right, but putting the answer in the wrong row.

# Strategies for the Performance Tasks

In this chapter, you'll find strategies that will give you a plan of attack for the performance tasks. In the next chapter (Chapter 5) you'll find a more specific step-by-step guide to each of the performance tasks. In Chapter 5 you'll find numerous tips relating to specific parts of the performance tasks as well as a number of pitfalls to avoid. These tips won't be repeated here; instead, this chapter focuses on broad strategies relating to how you plan and carry out the performance tasks.

## Strategy #1: Plan Your Project Before You Begin

Before each performance task officially begins with the required in-class time allocated to the project, be sure you think through what you will do. Your teacher has more leeway in answering questions before the project officially begins. You can ask questions about possible Explore and Create projects and get general advice. Your teacher may have your class do practice Explore and Create projects prior to the ones that you will submit to the College Board. Take advantage of this to fully understand the performance task expectations. Practicing and planning before you officially begin each of the performance tasks is a key to doing well.

In fact, it's never too early to start thinking about the Explore performance task, which requires you to research a computing innovation and create a computational artifact that explains its purpose. Well before your teacher officially gives you the eight official hours of class time required for this project, you should have chosen a topic and thought it through. Plan what you might do and ask your teacher any questions you have about the topic or your methodology. Be sure you'll be able to find recent enough sources to meet the requirement that at least two of your sources were created since the end of the previous academic year.

Remember that once you begin the actual eight-hour time period for the Explore performance task, you are more on your own and your teacher is more limited in the help that can be given. Your teacher can answer general questions related to the project task, timeline, components, and scoring; he or she cannot answer questions about the details of your specific topic. But for both the Explore and Create performance tasks, don't hesitate to ask any question you have; your teacher will decide if the question can be answered wholly, in part, or not at all.

The Create performance task requires you to develop a computer program, submit a video of the program running, and answer questions about the program you created. You should begin this task only after you have a good understanding of abstraction, algorithms, and programming since all three of these topics will be incorporated in your program and the written response.

However, here too, you should choose a topic and think it through before your AP class begins the 12 official hours of class time required for the Create performance task. Be sure your programming topic is broad enough to be able to meet the criteria of combining algorithms but not too broad so you cannot finish it on time. Before the task officially begins, you can plan what you want to do, discuss it with your partner (if you are collaborating), and ask your teacher questions about the topic or your planned methodology. But once the 12-hour time period begins, your teacher is more limited in what help can be given. After the project officially begins your teacher can only answer questions relating to the performance task in general.

## Strategy #2: Collaborate with a Classmate

The AP Computer Science Principles assessment is unique among AP exams in that it allows you to work with another student in your class. Take advantage of this and make it part of your strategy. Creating a computer program is the central requirement for the Create performance task. Programming is almost always better if people work together on it.

Keep in mind, though, that the collaboration allowed is limited to the programming that needs to be created for the Create performance task. Collaboration is not allowed on the Explore performance task. And even for the Create task, collaboration is limited to the development of the computer program that you need to create. Each of you will need to write sections of code independently, create your own video of the program running, and work on your own to complete the written responses.

Well before the 12-hour time period in your AP class for the Create performance task, you should try to line up a partner with whom you work well. You should talk about what type of program you want to create and plan what each of you will do. Make sure you are both on the same page with all of this before you officially begin to work together during the 12-hour in-class period. Also, be sure to plan enough time at the end to get the individual parts you each wrote integrated into the project and tested as a whole.

Don't worry if you are unable to line up a partner or simply prefer to work alone. Collaboration is encouraged, but not required.

## Strategy #3: Evaluate and Then Edit Your Written Responses

While the AP Computer Science Principles Exam is unique in that you'll find no free-response questions on the exam on test day (just multiple-choice questions), the test-makers have made up for this by including a number of free-response questions for both the Create and the Explore performance tasks. How you do on the written responses will determine most of your score on these performance tasks. With both the performance tasks, be sure to leave enough time to write the written response. You can have an excellent computational artifact (Explore task) or an amazing programming project (Create task), but if you do not write adequately about it, you will not receive points for it.

A key to getting a high score on both of the performance tasks is to carefully edit your written responses. The next chapter contains a step-by-step guide to answering the written responses. As you will discover, there are strict limits on the number of words you can use for each of the free-response questions. So, first, you'll need to edit your written responses to make sure they fall within the word-count limit for each question. But, to really improve your score, you'll have to take the editing one step further: You'll have to evaluate your answers based on the scoring rubric the College Board has provided and then edit your responses to pick up any points you've missed.

The College Board has made public the rubrics used to grade the written responses. These rubrics are included in the College Board's PDF document, "Assessment Overview and Performance Task Directions for Students." If you haven't already printed or bookmarked this document (mentioned in Chapter 1 and frequently referenced in Chapter 5), you can find it at this link:

https://apcentral.collegeboard.org/pdf/ap-csp-student-task-directions.pdf?course=ap-computer-science-principles

This scoring rubric is complex but very specific on how points are rewarded. Think of it as an "answer sheet" and use it to evaluate each of your written responses. By applying the "answer sheet" to your written responses, you can discover how many points each response would earn. More importantly, you can find out exactly what you need to add to your written response to earn any points you've missed. Edit your responses to pick up these points, being sure to remain within the word count limit for each question.

The College Board site also has helpful information in the form of samples of actual student responses for both the Explore and Create performance tasks. These examples are followed by a discussion of how points were awarded based on the rubric. You can follow these examples in evaluating your own written responses. These examples with scoring explanations can be found at:

> https://apcentral.collegeboard.org/courses/ap-computer-science-principles/
> exam?course=ap-computer-science-principles

Of course, evaluating your written responses based on the rubric and then editing your responses to match the rubric will take more time. You may not have time to complete this during the official 8- or 12-hour in-class time allocations. But there is no reason you can't continue working on this after the official minimum time period is over. You are permitted to spend more time outside of class to complete this task. The higher score you receive will be well worth the extra time you put in.

Now you are armed with the strategies that will help you attack and master the AP Computer Science Principles assessment. The next chapter focuses on the specifics of the Explore and Create performance tasks.

STEP 4

# Review the Knowledge You Need to Score High

# CHAPTER 5

# Creativity and the Performance Tasks

Big Idea # 1 of the AP Computer Science Principles Course

**IN THIS CHAPTER**

**Summary:** Creativity is a central part of the AP Computer Science Principles course but it is not assessed on the multiple-choice exam. Instead, it is demonstrated in the performance tasks that account for 40% of your overall AP score. For the Explore performance task you will need to research a computing innovation, create a computational artifact, and answer questions about that artifact. For the Create performance task you will need to create programing code, create a video showing the program running, and answer questions about the program you created.

**Key Ideas**

✪ Creativity is not assessed on the multiple-choice exam. Instead it is demonstrated on the Explore and Create performance tasks that together account for 40% of your AP score.
✪ The Explore performance task requires you to research a computing innovation, create a computational artifact, and provide a written response to questions.
✪ The Create performance task requires you create a computer program, create a video showing the program running, and provide a written response to questions.

**Key Terms**

Abstraction
Algorithm
API
Collaboration

Computational artifact
Computing innovation
Library
Software

# Creativity in Computer Science

Computer science is full of opportunities to be creative. Creativity is a way to express your personal ideas, selections of color combinations, fonts, wording, and images—among countless other options. There are numerous design decisions needed for a programming application to be easy to use and interesting to view. For example, creativity is essential for the development of entertainment software so that people will want to use their time and possibly spend their money to view or play this software.

Many people have their own method or process to follow to get their creative juices flowing. This can be a traditional process, such as an outline a writer might follow, or it can be an unconventional approach. Both methods can create entirely new artifacts or create a new artifact from combining all or parts of existing artifacts. It usually takes an iterative process to get from an idea to the actual creation in whatever form it takes. These processes can be used to find new solutions to problems as well as to create something of the creator's choosing.

## Creating Computational Artifacts

A computer artifact is anything created by a person using a computer. These include, but are not limited to, apps, games, images, videos, audio files, 3-D printed objects, and websites. Sometimes, learning a new software tool and experimenting with the different features the software provides can result in a creative and unexpected artifact.

There is a great deal of software available to use to create your own computational artifacts, from audio and visual files to mobile apps and everything in between. These software programs allow the creation and continued refining of artifacts from lower-levels of detail to highly precise ones. Depending on the ultimate planned outcome, software tools can provide an opportunity to create a sample or working prototype prior to investing the time and money required to create a physical copy of the artifact.

Companies will often task a team with creating an artifact. Effective collaboration requires good communication and conflict resolution processes to achieve the desired output, or product. There are many online tools that can help with collaboration, especially when team members are in different locations. While the artifact may have weaknesses or issues, the inclusion of everyone's ideas, experiences, and skills in the ultimate product usually results in a quality outcome. The evaluation of the artifact will help identify flaws that may be inherent in it or show up when the artifact is used in certain ways.

# Performance Tasks: The Basics

As you probably remember from Chapter 1, the AP Computer Science Principles Exam score is comprised of three factors:

1. The two-hour multiple-choice exam of 74 questions makes up 60% of the score.
2. The Explore performance task consists of submission of an artifact the student created along with a written response to research done on an innovative computing topic. It accounts for 16% of the final score.

3. The Create performance task is a program created by the student individually or through collaborating with another student along with a written response about it. This counts for 24% of the final score.

The artifacts created for the performance tasks must be uploaded to the College Board Digital Portfolio portal by the due date at the end of April. Students not attending a traditional school should contact the AP coordinator at their assigned school or at the school district level for information on how to register for the exam and submit their performance task projects.

The rubrics for grading both the Explore and Create performance tasks do not have a specific category for creativity. However, note that the description of creativity presented above includes collaboration and the use of software tools in creating computational artifacts along with an individual's creative process for developing the artifact and problem solving. These skills will be among those you'll use—and be evaluated on—in the performance tasks.

---

The College Board's document, "Assessment Overview and Performance Task Directions for Students," provides more information about the requirements for completing both the Explore and Create performance tasks. This PDF document was referenced in Chapter 4. If you haven't already printed or bookmarked this document, here is the link again:

https://apcentral.collegeboard.org/pdf/ap-csp-student-task-directions.pdf?course=ap-computer-science-principles

The College Board site also has examples of both Explore and Create projects along with their grading and an explanation of why each project received the scores it did (see the "Commentary" column). These projects can be viewed at:

https://apcentral.collegeboard.org/courses/ap-computer-science-principles/exam?course=ap-computer-science-principles

---

Be sure to look at the examples of the Explore and Create performance tasks that the College Board has provided online (see box above). Taking a careful look at these projects will be one of the most helpful things you can do to prepare yourself for the performance tasks. For each example there is the score the project received and an explanation of how it was evaluated.

# The Explore Performance Task

For the Explore performance task, you must find and research a computing innovation. Be sure to find one with a computational aspect to it. There are many innovations available, and some may appear to have a technology aspect to them, but be sure it is one that includes running software as part of its processing.

You will have eight hours of in-class time to work on the Explore task. You may use additional time outside of class, but all students will have at least eight hours to ensure everyone has adequate access to devices and the Internet to complete the Explore task. As explained in Chapter 4, your teacher is limited in the degree of assistance that can be provided and can only answer questions related to the Explore project task, timeline, components, and scoring in general and not about your project.

Teachers are limited in the type of questions they can answer regarding individual projects, especially after the official in-class time to complete the task has begun. But don't hesitate to ask a question you have for both the Explore and Create performance tasks. Your teacher will decide whether the question can be answered wholly, in part, or not at all.

You must work independently and create and use your own work. You cannot submit a project you may have worked on in class as a practice Explore project. No collaboration is allowed on the Explore performance task.

When choosing a computational innovation to research for the Explore performance task, be sure to pick a topic with recent enough sources so you can meet the requirement that at least two of your sources were created within the current academic year.

## Computational Artifact

To explain the purpose of the innovation you research, you will need to create a computational artifact about it. This artifact can be a video, audio file, or pdf. If you create a video or audio file, it must be a maximum of 60 seconds long and it must be less than 30 MB in size. There are several file formats that are acceptable. As of this writing, this list includes .mp3, .mp4, .wmv, .avi, .mov, .wav, aif, or .pdf format. Check the College Board's document, "Assessment Overview and Performance Task Directions for Students," (see the box above) for the most current list of acceptable file formats.

You may need to compress the file you create before uploading it to the College Board. Files that are too large will not upload to the College Board Digital Portfolio site. If you create a pdf, then it is limited to a maximum of three pages.

## Written Response

In addition, you must submit a written response to question prompts. The written response contains five sections, labeled 2.a, 2.b, 2.c, 2.d, and 2.e. Be sure to clearly label each one of your responses so the AP reader will know which question you are answering. You have a limit of 700 words to answer questions 2.a–2.d. Be sure to read each question carefully and make sure you answer it. Section 2.e is where you cite your sources and these are *not* included in the 700-word count. There are word count maximums for each section that comprise the 700 total word count:

- 2.a – maximum 100 words
- 2.b – maximum 100 words
- 2.c – maximum 250 words
- 2.d – maximum 250 words

Be sure to leave enough time to complete the written response. You can have an excellent computational artifact, but if you do not write adequately about it, you will not receive points for it. The grading focuses on your written responses, not on how cool the artifact is.

### Section 2.a

This section describes both the computing innovation and the computational artifact you created. In 100 words or less, include all of the following:

- **Name** of the computing innovation

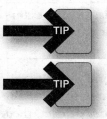

> Be sure to state what the innovation is. Many students lose this point because they never said what it was.

- The computing innovation's **purpose and function**

> Do *not* demonstrate a feature of the innovation rather than stating its purpose or function.

- A description of **how** the artifact you created represents the innovation's purpose or function

If you narrate or have captions on a video or pdf, or you create an audio recording as your artifact that answers 2.a, then the written response for question 2.a is not required. (In that case, total maximum word count declines to 600.)

Be sure to include a **fact** about the computing innovation's purpose or function. Do **not** write about the effect of the innovation here. That should be included in section 2.c. The fact about the innovation can be in your narration, in your captions, or written on your artifact or it can be in the 2.a written response if you did not include the other options with your artifact.

The computational artifact earns a point and the fact about the innovation's purpose earns a point.

## Section 2.b

In this section, you describe in detail the steps you took to create your computational artifact. Include the tools you used to create the artifact and enough detail so that someone unfamiliar with the tool could follow your process. You have a maximum of 100 words.

## Section 2.c

You can earn up to three points in this section, and you have a maximum of 250 words. Plan to use most of these words, and make them count. This section allows more than double the word count of what is allowed in other sections, indicating its importance.

The first point is awarded if you identify an **effect** of the computing innovation. You do not have to describe the effect or state if it is beneficial or harmful to earn this first point. However, you should go ahead and identify it as one or the other as the next point you can earn requires the effects to be identified as harmful or beneficial.

The second point is earned if you describe one beneficial **and** one harmful effect the computing innovation has already had or could have. Be sure the effects that you list are plausible and likely to occur. Note that if you earn this point, you will also earn the prior point.

> The AP reader will not try to interpret what you mean or guess which effect you are referencing, so be clear!

> Be sure to **use** the words *beneficial* and *harmful* when applicable (or a synonym) and clearly state which effect is or could be beneficial and which one is or could be harmful.

> **PITFALL TO AVOID:** Be sure to describe an effect here, not the purpose or function of the innovation. The purpose is the goal the innovation is expecting to achieve. The effect is the actual result, and it could be a positive outcome or effect or a negative one.

> **PITFALL TO AVOID:** Do not list hacking as a potential harmful effect unless the device is one designed to hack. For example, if robot bees are hacked, they could swarm a person and cause an accident. Since their purpose does not involve hacking, this would not be considered a reasonable harmful effect.

The third point is earned if an explanation is provided about how one of the effects—either the beneficial or harmful one—relates to our society, economy, *or* culture. For example, if the robot bee is the innovation, the benefit to culture could be the continued enjoyment of flowers because the flowers will be pollinated and continue to produce seeds. If the effect helps society do something like help people communicate better or get healthier and live longer, then it's a benefit. If the converse is true, then the innovation could end up being harmful to society, even though it is not the goal of the innovation. If the economy could be improved, or more jobs created, then the economy would be positively impacted. If the innovation could replace workers, then the economy could be negatively impacted. The digital divide and equal access to technology to take advantage of the innovation could be a factor here.

### Section 2.d

You will be writing about the data used by the computing innovation in this section. You have a maximum of 250 words, and two points can be earned.

To earn the first point, you must state what data is used and how the data is input, processed, or output. Clearly describe the data. Is it names, longitude and latitude coordinates, or temperature readings?

Then, you can describe how data is accessed, transformed, *or* produced by the innovation. If you discuss the input, be sure to describe how the data is accessed by the innovation. Does it have a sensor that transmits the data to the innovation? Is there a microphone that sends audio files to the innovation? Remember that the sensor and microphone are NOT the data; they are devices that take readings and sounds that can then be sent to the innovation.

If you choose to discuss how the innovation processes the data, do so clearly. For example, if temperature readings are sent as input, your computing innovation may process these readings by using software to compare each one to a low or high temperature.

If you write about output, then as our temperature example continues, state that as output, for temperature readings that are too high, an alert is sounded or a message is sent to the phone numbers registered with the software, and the thermostat is automatically lowered by a specified number of degrees. Your output could be one event or multiple events as in the example. Be clear about what occurs and what information is sent as output.

> **PITFALL TO AVOID:** Many students did not earn this point on last year's exam because they did not specify what the data was, and only said "data." If the data is a color, distance, image, temperature, or anything else, clearly state it.

The second point is awarded if you include either one data storage concern, one data privacy concern, *or* a data security concern that is caused directly by the computing innovation. For example, if your innovation takes in or produces large quantities of data, then storage could be a concern. If the data must be stored off-site, then the security of the data transmissions to and from the storage location could be a concern. Privacy could be a concern if the data was intercepted and personal information, such as credit card data, could be accessed. In your discussion, be sure to include *why* it is a concern.

**PITFALL TO AVOID:** Be sure the concern you address is related to the data and not another aspect of the innovation.

The AP reader will not guess or infer what you mean, so be specific about the concern you discuss and how the innovation impacts it.

### Section 2.e

You must cite at least three different sources, and two of them must be within the past academic year. The innovation can be older than that, but there must be current documentation about it for your research. Two of the three sources must be in either online or print form. The third source could be an interview with an expert, or it could be an additional digital or print source.

For online sources, you must document the URL, the author, title, source or publication, the date it was accessed, and the date it was written, if available.

Print sources must be cited with the author, the title of the publication (e.g., what magazine or book), page numbers, publisher, and date of publication.

If you conducted an interview, include the person's name, the date of the interview, and the person's position relative to the innovation, to indicate what makes the person an expert.

You must provide an in-text citation for each source in addition to the list of sources in this section. Some or all of the in-text citations can also be provided in the artifact, as well as in the written response.

The citation page in section 2.e does not need to follow a particular citation format, such as that of the *MLA Style Manual* or American Psychological Association (APA).

The in-text citations do not need to follow a particular format. Be sure to clearly indicate which source the in-text citation is referring to. You can use the author's last name or the number of the source if you clearly numbered them in section 2.e.

# The Create Performance Task

The Create performance task requires you to demonstrate both your programming knowledge and your creativity. You get to design and develop a program on a topic of your choice. You also get to select the programming language to use. No other AP exam even comes close to allowing you this much choice in what you want to do!

Students are encouraged to collaborate with another student on this task, but it is not required. If you do work with a partner, each student must complete some sections individually, and both must clearly identify sections created individually, by their partner, and those that were worked on together.

Twelve hours of class time must be provided to ensure all students have the same standard amount of time to create and document their project. You will have to turn in a video, a written response to question prompts, and the program code to the College Board Digital Portfolio portal.

As with the Explore performance task, teachers can only provide minimal assistance. You may ask them about the task and submission requirements or for help identifying a topic, resolving technical issues (such as connecting to a network), or saving files. You can also ask for help if a partner is not completing their work and for help with the correct usage of code from an application programming interface (API).

> Be sure your programming topic for the Create performance task is broad enough to be able to meet the criteria of combining algorithms but not too broad that you cannot finish it in time.

## Video Requirements

### Section 1

You have to submit a video of the program running. At least one function must be shown working, even if it is not working correctly. Show one that is key to the functioning of the program. If you narrate or use video captions, be sure to state the program's overall purpose, describe the function that is shown, and tell which programming language you used.

As with the Explore performance task, the video can be no more than 60 seconds long, no larger than 30 MB, and must be in one of the accepted file formats. As of this writing, these are .mp4, .wmv, .avi, or .mov. Check the College Board's document, "Assessment Overview and Performance Task Directions for Students," for the most current list of acceptable file formats. (If you haven't already printed or bookmarked this PDF document, see the box earlier in this chapter for information on accessing it.)

> **PITFALL TO AVOID:** Even if you work with a partner, you each must create your own video.

## Written Response Requirements

You have a maximum of 750 words total to answer the prompts. Be sure to clearly label them, and be direct about answering the question asked. That is not many words to get your ideas across, so ensure your writing is succinct and clear.

> Be sure to leave plenty of time to complete the written response. You can write an amazing program, but if you do not write adequately about it to answer all the questions, you will not receive many points for it. The grading focuses mostly on your written responses, not on how cool your programming is.

### Section 2.a

You must include the program's purpose, state the programming language used, and describe the function that was shown in the video. If you narrate or caption your video and provide this information in that format, then you do not need to complete this section in writing. Otherwise, you have a maximum of 150 words. If you do not write a response for this section, you have a maximum of 600 words for the rest of the written responses combined.

### Section 2.b

This section can earn two points toward your overall score if done properly. You have a maximum of 200 words to answer this prompt.

One point can be earned if you describe the iterative steps used to develop your application. While you do not have to use a formal software development process, you do need to clearly describe the iterations you used. Software is developed by defining the requirements, designing a solution, coding the solution, and then testing it and repeating the steps. You need to document how, after testing, you improved the program by refining the design based on a better understanding of the requirements or based on feedback about how easy the program was to use or how well it functioned, or correcting programming errors. Be sure you discuss your evaluation and reflection of the results and thoughts about how to improve your program for the next iteration.

> You must document more than two iterations to earn this point.

You can earn another point in your response to section 2.b if you describe two instances in your development process that you had to resolve either opportunities or problems. You can describe two opportunities, two problems, or one of each. Then you *must* include the resolution of the two you shared to earn the point.

### Section 2.c
You can earn up to three points in this section and have up to 200 words.

Remember that an algorithm is a set of steps to complete a task. The **first point** is earned by identifying an algorithm in a section of code that you wrote *independently*. Take a screen clipping of these algorithms and paste it in this section of your write-up.

> **PITFALL TO AVOID:** The algorithm chosen can use an API or library call you imported into your program, but cannot be only the API code. It also must be longer than one instruction (e.g., DISPLAY or PRINT would not be acceptable).

> Be sure to select an algorithm you wrote independently, not with a partner.

The second point is earned when one of the algorithms selected uses math or logical concepts. The math functions can be shown with any of the arithmetic operators, such as +, -, *, /, MOD, or mathematical functions, such as finding the square root, or generating a random number. Logical concepts include Boolean conditions. Remember that Boolean conditions evaluate to either true or false. The logical concepts used can include the "AND", "OR", and "NOT" operators to create compound conditions. In this section, you must explain how this algorithm works and what its purpose is in the program as a whole.

> This algorithm does not have to be completely written by the student. It can include code that was imported into the program via a library call as part of an algorithm.

> **PITFALL TO AVOID:** Be sure to write about what the algorithm does **and** how it does it plus its role in the overall program functionality.

The third point is earned if the selected algorithm is made up of at least two or more algorithms. As an example, you could have a selection of code that includes an algorithm to ask the user for input, such as a response to a question like "Do you want to play a game?" An algorithm could check the response for valid input and print an error message if it is not valid. If it is a valid choice, a third algorithm could keep score, and use the mathematical expressions to keep score. Another algorithm could see if the score is a new high score, which could use the Boolean operators in the comparison. All of these algorithms have an independent function, and used together can help make a game.

> Be sure to include how one of the algorithms functions independently in addition to how it combines with the other algorithms.

Section 3 (see below) contains a copy of your entire program. You *must* also place an oval shape around the algorithms you select. You **cannot** use your entire program as the algorithm.

> The discussion about the algorithms, the section of code pasted in this section, and the oval shape around it in section 3 must be present to earn the points.

### Section 2.d

This section has a maximum of 200 words and requires students to identify an abstraction they wrote independently. Examples of abstractions can be procedures, parameters, lists, APIs, or libraries. Remember you need to have written the code, so you may call a library or API, but it cannot make up the entire abstraction. It must contain mathematical or logic structures, like the algorithm did. The math or logic structure could include processing a list to find the element that is the largest, smallest, oldest, newest, or count how many elements of the list contain a certain number or letter, or any other condition to check each element in the list.

Take a screen clipping of the abstraction and include it here. You must also place a rectangle around the abstraction in the complete code included in section 3. Be sure it is the one you are writing about in this section.

> Using procedures with or without parameters can be a good example of an abstraction. Creating a list to represent an existing abstraction in your program would also earn the point. An example could be creating a list to identify all the turtle nests in a location for the year.

> **PITFALL TO AVOID:** Do not select the entire program as your abstraction example.

> **PITFALL TO AVOID:** Be sure to use the correct shape around the abstraction (rectangle) and algorithm (oval).

The second point is earned by explaining **how** the abstraction helps to simplify aspects of your program. If the abstraction is a procedure, then it helps simplify or generalize that function so it can be called multiple times in the program. This avoids duplicating code every time you need to do that process. Once a procedure is tested and working, you no longer have to think about the code itself. You merely need to "call" the procedure to execute it.

If a procedure has parameters, these work to simplify the process by allowing different data to be sent to the procedure. This makes it more useful for more sets of data the program may need to process. Again, the code can stay hidden in the procedure, and different values can be sent to it each time.

### Section 3

This section includes your **entire** code in PDF format. The algorithms are marked with an oval and the abstractions are marked by a rectangle. This is where you acknowledge who wrote sections of code that you did not, whether it was your partner or through use of an imported library.

Keeping programming notes to document design decisions and programming structures as you implement algorithms and incorporate abstraction will help in writing the written response for this section. You can also record issues that came up and how they were resolved.

You are encouraged to work with a partner on this project, even though you both must also independently create sections of code and you each must work independently to create your own video and written responses. Remember that you cannot submit a project you may have worked on in class as a practice Create project.

Always refer to College Board's document "Assessment Overview and Performance Task Directions for Students" for specific details on the code and written response expectations. If you haven't already bookmarked or printed this document, here is the link again:

https://apcentral.collegeboard.org/pdf/ap-csp-student-task-directions.pdf?course=ap-computer-science-principles

# Submitting Your Performance Tasks to the College Board

To submit your Explore and Create performance tasks, you must have an account on the College Board Digital Portfolio site. The link is:

https://digitalportfolio.collegeboard.org/

If you took an AP class in a prior year, you will already have an account. Be sure to use this same account. If you cannot remember your username or password, you can click the "Forgot username or password" options, and a message will be sent to the email address you registered with.

Once you have logged in, request to join the class your teacher has set up. Your teacher will then approve your request and your account will be ready to accept the performance tasks.

Independent study students must contact the AP coordinator at their assigned school or their school district. Students must be registered in an approved class in the College Board digital portfolio website. This is where the Explore and Create performance tasks are uploaded. If you do not have a local school to contact, please call the College Board at 1-877-274-6474.

Each performance task is broken down into separate parts you must upload:

**Explore Performance Task**
This section has two components:
- Computational Artifact—labeled CA
- Written Response—labeled WR

**Create Performance Task**
This section has three components:
- Individual Video—labeled IV
- Individual Written Response—labeled IWR
- Program Code—labeled PC

Until you load a submission, the components are labelled with a gray square. □ After you submit a section, the shape will show an orange triangle. You may still upload new versions at this time. △ After you submit as final, you cannot overlay a new version anymore and a check mark shows ✔. However, your instructor may return a file to you after final submission. The teacher has to indicate one of the valid reasons for returning the final submission. No files can be returned after the submission date passes.

> Be sure you are uploading Explore components in the Explore section and Create components in the Create section. Students sometimes upload to the wrong performance task. You can still overlay the task with a new one, but you cannot delete the initial one you loaded.

> **PITFALL TO AVOID:** You cannot have a file with the same name in both the Create and Explore sections. The portfolio portal will not allow you to upload a file with the same name as one you already submitted. Students sometimes label their written responses the same. Just be aware of this and ensure they have different names, such as wrC for written response Create and wrE for written response Explore.

> Be sure to check that you plan to take the multiple-choice exam while you are in the digital portfolio as well.

> Be sure to submit your performance task sections before the due date to avoid delay in the event the site slows down or becomes unavailable due to high demand. Plan to finish and submit your projects before the due date in late April. This date is set by the College Board each year and can be found on their website.

If you cannot complete all aspects of the Explore and Create performance tasks before the submission deadline, you may still submit the sections you have completed to the College Board portal. They will be graded. You will only receive points for the sections that were submitted.

# ❯ Rapid Review

A computational artifact is anything created by a person using a computer. This includes videos, podcasts, 3-D printed objects, games, and apps, among many others.

The Explore and Create performance tasks must be uploaded to the College Board digital portfolio site by the due date set by the College Board each year. It is usually near the end of April.

Review the examples and rubrics on the College Board site. Grade your own project based on the rubric and modify as needed before your final submission to the College Board.

Be aware of the maximum word counts for each section of your written responses for the performance tasks.

AP readers will not guess or try to infer what you mean, so be specific in your written responses.

# CHAPTER 6

# Abstraction

Big Idea # 2 of the AP Computer Science Principles Course

## IN THIS CHAPTER

**Summary:** Abstraction is a key concept with both hardware and software. Details are removed to focus on the essential aspects. We can then focus on what the abstractions do, not how they do them.

### Key Ideas

- ✪ Abstractions are created by removing details and making concepts more general.
- ✪ Abstractions including numbers, colors, text, and instructions can be represented by binary data.
- ✪ Numbers can be converted from one number system to another.
- ✪ Software applications are built from hardware and software abstractions.
- ✪ Abstractions can be combined to create programs.
- ✪ Models and simulations are abstractions to test theories in a safer, controlled, and faster environment.

**Key Terms**

Abstraction
ASCII table
Binary
Bit
Byte
Hardware architecture
Hexadecimal
Hierarchal
Logic gate

Model
Octal
Overflow
Parameter
Procedure
Round-off or Rounding
   error
Simulator

# What Is an Abstraction?

Abstraction is a concept that is a little hard for many students to grasp. The basic idea is we remove details to make something more general. This makes it easier to use the process for multiple purposes versus one specific purpose. One benefit is that we do not have to know what goes on behind the scenes, meaning how it works. We only need to know that it works.

### Examples of Non-Coding Abstractions

A light switch is an example of an abstraction. The details are reduced and all we have to do is flip the switch on or off. We do not need to know the details of what is going on when the switch is up and current flows through the circuit. The switch concept works for many different kinds of lights and other devices, such as turning on a coffee pot.

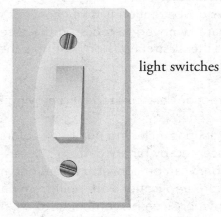

light switches

Computer Science is full of abstractions. We reduce or generalize the details to be able to use the code for multiple purposes.

### Examples of Coding Abstractions

The "print" or "DISPLAY" commands in a programming language are an abstraction. We only have to say "print" or "DISPLAY" along with what to show either on the computer screen or to print on paper. It is flexible in that we can print text, numbers or expressions to evaluate before printing the result. We do not have to know how the procedures work in any particular programming language.

```
print("Hello World!")
DISPLAY(5)
DISPLAY("The temperature is:", temperature)
print ("The average is:", (t1 + t2 + t3)/3)
```

When you tap or click on a button in a mobile app, code is executed and information or features are displayed or changed. We do not need to know what the code is or how it works, only that it does what we expect when the button is pressed, so the button is the abstraction.

Calculators work the same way. When we click values and operations to perform on them, we do not know how the mathematical operations are being handled inside the calculator. We see the result displayed and know we can trust it.

## Numbers as Abstractions

Think of several ways you can represent the number of marbles in the pile in the image.

8, eight, ocho
VIII (Roman numerals)

卌 Ⅲ

Each of these is a simplified way to represent how many marbles are in the pile. Each numeric representation is an abstraction, because they simplify the details of what we have, and we know that we have "eight" of them. Each of the different number systems represents the same amount. Other number systems can also be used.

Binary and hexadecimal are the most common number systems used in computer science. Computers read machine code, which at the lowest level, is made up of 0s and 1s. This is the binary number system. A "0" represents no electrical charge and "1" represents a charge. "Current" and "no current" are easy conditions to detect. These binary digits are referred to as bits.

Since this is a digital document, the image of the marbles is also represented by binary digits, 0s and 1s. We see the image of the marbles and do not need to know how the shapes and colors are represented by the bits. The words on this page are represented by bits, 0s and 1s. All digital data are represented by different abstractions such as these.

We need to understand hexadecimal, base 16, because it is often used by people, not computers, to represent a shorter version of a binary number. Computers still use binary, and these binary numbers get very long very quickly. Since hexadecimal uses 16 numbers, more numbers can be represented with fewer digits than binary can. Octal, base 8, numbers were previously used in older computers, but the hexadecimal system has replaced it over time since more numbers can be represented with fewer digits.

# Number Systems and Place Value

All number systems use the same principles.

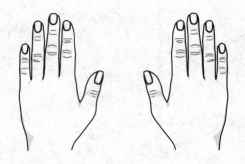

Our base 10 **decimal** system uses 10 numbers from 0 – 9.

When you need the number 10, you have to carry over to a new column, the "tens" column, and use 2 numbers. Your number represents how many "tens" you have and how many "ones" you have. When you need to represent the number "100", you have to carry over to a third column, the "hundreds" column.

Each new column represents the next power of 10.

| $10^3$ | $10^2$ | $10^1$ | $10^0$ |
|---|---|---|---|
| Thousands | Hundreds | Tens | Ones |
| 1000 | 100 | 10 | 1 |

Base 2, **binary**, uses two numbers, 0 and 1.
When you need the number 2, you have to carry over to a new column, the "twos", and use 2 numbers to represent it. Your number represents how many "twos" you have and how many "ones" you have. For the number "4", you carry over to a third column, the "fours". The next column is the "eights".
Each new column to the left represents the next power of 2.

| $2^3$ | $2^2$ | $2^1$ | $2^0$ |
|---|---|---|---|
| Eights | Fours | Twos | Ones |
| 8 | 4 | 2 | 1 |

## Converting Decimal Numbers to Binary

When you need to convert a decimal number to binary, create the following table on your paper.

| $2^7$ | $2^6$ | $2^5$ | $2^4$ | $2^3$ | $2^2$ | $2^1$ | $2^0$ |
|---|---|---|---|---|---|---|---|
| 128 | 64 | 32 | 16 | 8 | 4 | 2 | 1 |

Notice that each column to the left represents an increasing power of 2 which doubles the column to the right of it.

To convert a decimal number to binary, use the following algorithm with the above table.

1. Write down the decimal number
2. Subtract the largest number from the binary table that is the same or less. (When you subtract, you cannot have a negative number.)
3. Mark a one in the column on the table for the power of 2 you subtracted.
4. Mark a zero in the columns that could not be subtracted and were skipped.
5. Repeat steps 2 – 4 until your decimal value reaches zero.
6. Note: Use leading "0's" on the left to make a byte (8 bits.)

### Example 1: Convert 21 to binary

Starting from the left-most column, the first number you can subtract without having a negative result is 16. Place a 0 in each column to the left of $2^4$ and a 1 in the column for $2^4$.

$$\begin{array}{r} 21 \\ -16 \\ \hline 5 \end{array}$$

Take the number remaining after subtracting and find the next number in the table that can be subtracted without resulting in a negative number.
You cannot subtract 8, so place a 0 in the $2^3$ column.
You can subtract 4, so place a 1 in the $2^2$ column.

$$\begin{array}{r} 5 \\ -4 \\ \hline 1 \end{array}$$

The result is now 1, so place a 1 in the $2^0$ column.

$$\begin{array}{r} 1 \\ -1 \\ \hline 0 \end{array}$$

Answer: $21_{10} = 00010101_2$

| $2^7$ | $2^6$ | $2^5$ | $2^4$ | $2^3$ | $2^2$ | $2^1$ | $2^0$ |
|---|---|---|---|---|---|---|---|
| 128 | 64 | 32 | 16 | 8 | 4 | 2 | 1 |
| 0 | 0 | 0 | 1 | 0 | 1 | 0 | 1 |

**Example 2: Convert 119 to binary**

Create your table of powers of 2 from $2^0$ to $2^7$.

Starting from the left-most column, the first number you can subtract without having a negative result is 64. Place a 0 in each column to the left of $2^6$ and a 1 in the column for $2^6$. Subtract the value of $2^6$ which is 64, from 119.

$$\begin{array}{r} 119 \\ -\ 64 \\ \hline 55 \end{array}$$

The next power of 2 is $2^5$ which is 32. This can be subtracted without a negative result, so place a 1 in the $2^5$ column.

$$\begin{array}{r} 55 \\ -32 \\ \hline 23 \end{array}$$

The next power of 2 is $2^4$ which is 16. This can be subtracted without a negative result, so place a 1 in the $2^4$ column

$$\begin{array}{r} 23 \\ -16 \\ \hline 7 \end{array}$$

We cannot subtract 8 and have a positive result, so place a 0 in the $2^3$ column. We can subtract 4, so place a 1 in the $2^2$ column.

$$\begin{array}{r} 7 \\ -4 \\ \hline 3 \end{array}$$

We can subtract 2 from 3, so place a 1 in the $2^1$ column.

$$\begin{array}{r} 3 \\ -2 \\ \hline 1 \end{array}$$

The result is now 1, so place a 1 in the $2^0$ column.

$$\begin{array}{r} 1 \\ -1 \\ \hline 0 \end{array}$$

The result of the conversion is:

$119_{10} = 01110111_2$

| $2^7$ | $2^6$ | $2^5$ | $2^4$ | $2^3$ | $2^2$ | $2^1$ | $2^0$ |
|---|---|---|---|---|---|---|---|
| 128 | 64 | 32 | 16 | 8 | 4 | 2 | 1 |
| 0 | 1 | 1 | 1 | 0 | 1 | 1 | 1 |

## Converting Binary Numbers to Decimal

To convert a binary number to decimal:

1. Write the binary table as we did in the examples above with each bit of the binary number in the appropriate column.
2. For columns that have a 1 in them, add the values of the power of 2.
   (You are multiplying 1 * the value of the power of 2 in each column.)
3. The total of all columns with a 1 in them equals the decimal value equivalent.

**Example 1: Convert "00011011" to decimal**

| $2^7$ | $2^6$ | $2^5$ | $2^4$ | $2^3$ | $2^2$ | $2^1$ | $2^0$ |
|---|---|---|---|---|---|---|---|
| 128 | 64 | 32 | 16 | 8 | 4 | 2 | 1 |
| 0 | 0 | 0 | 1 | 1 | 0 | 1 | 1 |
| 0 + | 0 + | 0 + | 1 * 16 + | 1 * 8 + | 0 + | 1 * 2 + | 1 * 1 = |

16 + 8 + 2 + 1 = 27

**Example 2: Convert 11011001 to decimal**

| $2^7$ | $2^6$ | $2^5$ | $2^4$ | $2^3$ | $2^2$ | $2^1$ | $2^0$ |
|---|---|---|---|---|---|---|---|
| 128 | 64 | 32 | 16 | 8 | 4 | 2 | 1 |
| 1 | 1 | 0 | 1 | 1 | 0 | 0 | 1 |
| 128 * 1+ | 64 * 1 + | 0 + | 1 * 16 + | 1 * 8 + | 0 + | 0 + | 1 * 1 = |

128 + 64 + 16 + 8 + 1 = 217

> Any time you have a binary number that is all "1's" to the right, the number in decimal is always 1 less than the next power of 2. Logically this makes sense, since you cannot have the number "2" in binary. The next value would need a new column and would be the next power of 2. For example:
>
> $00000111_2 = 7_{10}$ because the next value in the chart would be $2^3 = 8$ or $1000_2$
>
> $00011111_2 = 31_{10}$ because the next column is $2^5$ or 32
>
> $01111111_2 = 127$ because the next column is $2^7$ or 128

## Converting Decimal Numbers to Hexadecimal

Hexadecimal representations work exactly the same way as binary and decimal do. Create a table with 16 raised to the power starting at 0. Note that each column can have a value from 0 – 15 in it with A – F representing 10 – 15.

### Example 1: Convert the decimal number 119 to hexadecimal

Divide 119 by the largest power of 16 that is less than 119. 119 / 16 = 7 with a remainder of 7. Place a 7 in the $16^1$ column. Since we have less than a power of 16 remaining, you place a 7 in the $16^0$ column.

Answer: $119_{10} = 77_{16}$

| $16^3$ | $16^2$ | $16^1$ | $16^0$ |
|---|---|---|---|
| 4096 | 256 | 16 | 1 |
| 0 | 0 | 7 | 7 |

### Example 2: Convert $2793_{10}$ to hexadecimal

**Step 1:** Divide by the largest power of 16 that is less than 2793.
2793 / 256 = 10 with a remainder of 233.

Normally we would place 10 in the $16^2$ column, but we can only have a single character represent a number. For hexadecimal, the letter A represents the number 10.

**Step 2:** Divide the remainder 233 by the largest power of 16 that is less than 233.

233 / 16 = 14 with a remainder of 9.

We cannot place 14 in the $16^1$ column since it is 2 digits. In hexadecimal, the letter E represents the value 14.

**Step 3:** We have the remainder of 9 left for the "ones" column. Place the number 9 in the $16^0$.

| $16^3$ | $16^2$ | $16^1$ | $16^0$ |
|---|---|---|---|
| 4096 | 256 | 16 | 1 |
| 0 | 10 → A | 14 → E | 9 |

Answer: $2793_{10} = AE9_{16}$

## Converting Binary Numbers to Hexadecimal

When you need to convert from binary to hexadecimal, there is a convenient shortcut to do this. Follow the steps below:

1. Separate your 8-bit binary number into two groups of 4 bits, starting from the right. You may add leading zeroes to the left grouping if needed.
2. Convert each group of four bits to their decimal equivalent. Note that 4 bits will give you a value between 0 – 15.
3. Remember that in hexadecimal, 10 – 15 are represented by the characters "A – F".

**Example 1: Convert 01011010 to hexadecimal**
**Step 1:** Separate the binary number into two groups of four bits each.

0101    1010

**Step 2:** Convert each group of four bits to its decimal equivalent: 0-15

0101 → 5    1010 → 10

**Step 3:** Remember you cannot have 2 digits, so convert 10-15 to their letter equivalent. The number 10 is "A" in hexadecimal.

Answer: $01011010_2 = 5A_{16}$

**Example 2: Convert 99 in decimal to hexadecimal**
**Step 1:** Convert 99 to binary. Set up the table of the powers of 2 convert to binary. See the section on converting decimal numbers to binary for details.

99 – 64 = 35 → place 1 in the $2^6$ column
35 – 32 =  3 → place 1 in the $2^5$ column
3 – 2 =  1 → place 1 in the $2^1$ column
1 – 1 =  0 → place 1 in the $2^0$ column

| $2^7$ | $2^6$ | $2^5$ | $2^4$ | $2^3$ | $2^2$ | $2^1$ | $2^0$ |
|---|---|---|---|---|---|---|---|
| 128 | 64 | 32 | 16 | 8 | 4 | 2 | 1 |
| 0 | 1 | 1 | 0 | 0 | 0 | 1 | 1 |

**Step 2:** Separate your binary number into two groups of 4 bits which will be a value between 0-15.

0110    0011

**Step 3:** Convert each group of bits to their decimal equivalent.

$$0110 \rightarrow 6 \qquad 0011 \rightarrow 3$$

Answer: $99_{10} = 01100011_2 = 63_{16}$

Here is a table with equivalent decimal, binary, and hexadecimal values. You do not need to memorize the table, but you should be able to convert numbers from one base to the next.

| Decimal | Hexadecimal | Binary |
|---------|-------------|----------|
| 0 | 0 | 00000000 |
| 1 | 1 | 00000001 |
| 2 | 2 | 00000010 |
| 3 | 3 | 00000011 |
| 4 | 4 | 00000100 |
| 5 | 5 | 00000101 |
| 6 | 6 | 00000110 |
| 7 | 7 | 00000111 |
| 8 | 8 | 00001000 |
| 9 | 9 | 00001001 |
| 10 | A | 00001010 |
| 11 | B | 00001011 |
| 12 | C | 00001100 |
| 13 | D | 00001101 |
| 14 | E | 00001110 |
| 15 | F | 00001111 |
| 16 | 10 | 00010000 |

# How Binary Numbers Can Be Interpreted

In addition to the numbers we just reviewed, binary numbers can also represent letters for text fields.

### ASCII

The table below is an example of an ASCII (American Standard Code for Information Interchange) table. ASCII is used to convert text to binary codes so computers can read it. These standard character sets use 7 bits. Therefore ASCII can only represent 128 characters from 0 - 127. It is no longer in widespread use as it has been replaced by the larger Unicode table which includes conversions for character-based languages, such as Chinese. However, the process is the same with both tables and the values for 0 to 127 are the same.

If you had the decimal value 65, you see that it equals 41 hexadecimal, and 1000001 in binary and the letter "A" as a character. Be sure you understand how to find a character in the table if you are given a binary number and to find the numbers, (binary or hexadecimal), if you are given a character or symbol.

The software for the particular application knows when it sees $01000001_2$ whether it is looking for a number or a letter and interprets it accordingly.

## ASCII Table

| Decimal | Hexa-decimal | Binary | Octal | Char | Decimal | Hexa-decimal | Binary | Octal | Char | Decimal | Hexa-decimal | Binary | Octal | Char |
|---|---|---|---|---|---|---|---|---|---|---|---|---|---|---|
| 0 | 0 | 0 | 0 | Null | 43 | 2B | 101011 | 53 | + | 86 | 56 | 1010110 | 126 | V |
| 1 | 1 | 1 | 1 | Start of Heading | 44 | 2C | 101100 | 54 | , | 87 | 57 | 1010111 | 127 | W |
| 2 | 2 | 10 | 2 | Start of Text | 45 | 2D | 101101 | 55 | - | 88 | 58 | 1011000 | 130 | Z |
| 3 | 3 | 11 | 3 | End of Text | 46 | 2E | 101110 | 56 | . | 89 | 59 | 1011001 | 131 | Y |
| 4 | 4 | 100 | 4 | End of Transmission | 47 | 2F | 101111 | 57 | / | 90 | 5A | 1011010 | 132 | Z |
| 5 | 5 | 101 | 5 | Enquiry | 48 | 30 | 110000 | 60 | 0 | 91 | 5B | 1011011 | 133 | [ |
| 6 | 6 | 110 | 6 | Acknowledge | 49 | 31 | 110001 | 61 | 1 | 92 | 5C | 1011100 | 134 | \ |
| 7 | 7 | 111 | 7 | Bell | 50 | 32 | 110010 | 62 | 2 | 93 | 5D | 1011101 | 135 | ] |
| 8 | 8 | 1000 | 10 | Backspace | 51 | 33 | 110011 | 63 | 3 | 94 | 5E | 1011110 | 136 | ^ |
| 9 | 9 | 1001 | 11 | Horizontal Tab | 52 | 34 | 110100 | 64 | 4 | 95 | 5F | 1011111 | 137 | _ |
| 10 | A | 1010 | 12 | Line Feed | 53 | 35 | 110101 | 65 | 5 | 96 | 60 | 1100000 | 140 | ` |
| 11 | B | 1011 | 13 | Vertical Tab | 54 | 36 | 110110 | 66 | 6 | 97 | 61 | 1100001 | 141 | a |
| 12 | C | 1100 | 14 | Form Feed | 55 | 37 | 110111 | 67 | 7 | 98 | 62 | 1100010 | 142 | b |
| 13 | D | 1101 | 15 | Carriage Return | 56 | 38 | 111000 | 70 | 8 | 99 | 63 | 1100011 | 143 | c |
| 14 | E | 1110 | 16 | Shift Out | 57 | 39 | 111001 | 71 | 9 | 100 | 64 | 1100100 | 144 | d |
| 15 | F | 1111 | 17 | Shift In | 58 | 3A | 111010 | 72 | : | 101 | 65 | 1100101 | 145 | e |
| 16 | 10 | 10000 | 20 | Data Link Escape | 59 | 3B | 111011 | 73 | ; | 102 | 66 | 1100110 | 146 | f |
| 17 | 11 | 10001 | 21 | Device Control 1 | 60 | 3C | 111100 | 74 | < | 103 | 67 | 1100111 | 147 | g |
| 18 | 12 | 10010 | 22 | Device Control 2 | 61 | 3D | 111101 | 75 | = | 104 | 68 | 1101000 | 150 | h |
| 19 | 13 | 10011 | 23 | Device Control 3 | 62 | 3E | 111110 | 76 | > | 105 | 69 | 1101001 | 151 | i |
| 20 | 14 | 10100 | 24 | Device Control 4 | 63 | 3F | 111111 | 77 | ? | 106 | 6A | 1101010 | 152 | j |
| 21 | 15 | 10101 | 25 | Negative Acknowledge | 64 | 40 | 1000000 | 100 | @ | 107 | 6B | 1101011 | 153 | k |
| 22 | 16 | 10110 | 26 | Synchronous Idle | 65 | 41 | 1000001 | 101 | A | 108 | 6C | 1101100 | 154 | l |
| 23 | 17 | 10111 | 27 | End of Trans. Block | 66 | 42 | 1000010 | 102 | B | 109 | 6D | 1101101 | 155 | m |
| 24 | 18 | 11000 | 30 | Cancel | 67 | 43 | 1000011 | 103 | C | 110 | 6E | 1101110 | 156 | n |
| 25 | 19 | 11001 | 31 | End of Medium | 68 | 44 | 1000100 | 104 | D | 111 | 6F | 1101111 | 157 | o |
| 26 | 1A | 11010 | 32 | Substitute | 69 | 45 | 1000101 | 105 | E | 112 | 70 | 1110000 | 160 | p |
| 27 | 1B | 11011 | 33 | Escape | 70 | 46 | 1000110 | 106 | F | 113 | 71 | 1110001 | 161 | q |
| 28 | 1C | 11100 | 34 | File Separator | 71 | 47 | 1000111 | 107 | G | 114 | 72 | 1110010 | 162 | r |
| 29 | 1D | 11101 | 35 | Group Separator | 72 | 48 | 1001000 | 110 | H | 115 | 73 | 1110011 | 163 | s |
| 30 | 1E | 11110 | 36 | Record Separator | 73 | 49 | 1001001 | 111 | I | 116 | 74 | 1110100 | 164 | t |
| 31 | 1F | 11111 | 37 | Unit Separator | 74 | 4A | 1001010 | 112 | J | 117 | 75 | 1110101 | 165 | u |
| 32 | 20 | 100000 | 40 | Space | 75 | 4B | 1001011 | 113 | K | 118 | 76 | 1110110 | 166 | v |
| 33 | 21 | 100001 | 41 | ! | 76 | 4C | 1001100 | 114 | L | 119 | 77 | 1110111 | 167 | w |
| 34 | 22 | 100010 | 42 | " | 77 | 4D | 1001101 | 115 | M | 120 | 78 | 1111000 | 170 | x |
| 35 | 23 | 100011 | 43 | # | 78 | 4E | 1001110 | 116 | N | 121 | 79 | 1111001 | 171 | y |
| 36 | 24 | 100100 | 44 | $ | 79 | 4F | 1001111 | 117 | O | 122 | 7A | 1111010 | 172 | z |
| 37 | 25 | 100101 | 45 | % | 80 | 50 | 1010000 | 120 | P | 123 | 7B | 1111011 | 173 | { |
| 38 | 26 | 100110 | 46 | & | 81 | 51 | 1010001 | 121 | Q | 124 | 7C | 1111100 | 174 | | |
| 39 | 27 | 100111 | 47 | ' | 82 | 52 | 1010010 | 122 | R | 125 | 7D | 1111101 | 175 | } |
| 40 | 28 | 101000 | 50 | ( | 83 | 53 | 1010011 | 123 | S | 126 | 7E | 1111110 | 176 | ~ |
| 41 | 29 | 101001 | 51 | ) | 84 | 54 | 1010100 | 124 | T | 127 | 7F | 1111111 | 177 | Del |
| 42 | 2A | 101010 | 52 | * | 85 | 55 | 1010101 | 125 | U | | | | | |

## Colors

Binary numbers are also used to represent colors. The human eye primarily detects red, green, and blue. Other colors are a combination of these three colors in different amounts. Computer monitors work the same way and add differing amounts of red, green, and blue to create the colors that are displayed. That is where RGB, for Red, Green, and Blue, came to be known and can still be seen as a label for monitor and projector connections.

Earlier color representations used a byte, (8 bits), for colors using three bits for red, three for green, and two for blue: RRRGGGBB. Only 128 colors could be represented using 1 byte.

Now, computers use one byte for each color. RRRRRRRRGGGGGGGGBBBBBBBB

With eight numbers for each color, we can create 256 possible shades of red *times* 256 possible green shades *times* 256 possible blue shades:

$$256 * 256 * 256 = 16,777,216 \text{ possible colors}$$

These would be very long binary numbers, so this is an example where both the decimal equivalent for each color and the hexadecimal equivalent are commonly used. Many online color charts use the hexadecimal representation for a color. Coding a color can be done with two hexadecimal digits each for red, green, and blue still providing 256 shades of each color and over 16 million possible colors.

Notice in the table below:

Black is zero amounts of red, green, and blue.

White is the full amounts of red, green, and blue.

Blue has the full amount of blue, but no other color.

**Color Chart Examples**

| Color Name | RGB (Red Green Blue) Triplet | Hexadecimal |
|---|---|---|
| Blue | (0, 0, 255) | 0000FF |
| Silver | (192, 192, 192) | C0C0C0 |
| Purple | (128, 0, 128) | 800080 |
| Ruby | (224, 17, 95) | E0115F |
| Emerald | (80, 200, 120) | 50C878 |
| Black | (0, 0, 0) | 000000 |
| White | (255, 255, 255) | FFFFFF |

Just as with text and numbers, the software program takes in the value and interprets it as a color, text value, or number, based on what the program is expecting.

## Machine Instructions

When your code is converted from the natural language type code, such as: print("Error!"), to machine language, it is converted to binary. Just as with numbers, text, and colors, the compiler or interpreter is software that knows how to convert the values and what they represent in binary.

```
print("Error!")
```

The text "Error!" is converted to binary as below.

01000101 01110010 01110010 01110010 01110010 00100001

The "print" command is also converted to binary along with the instructions in binary that tell the program how to print text.

In summary, if we simply had a binary number: 00101001, we would not know what it represented. It could be a number, text, color, or instruction. However, the software using it knows what it represents.

# Processing Binary Data

Binary data is processed by hardware.

### Logic Gates/Chips

Logic gates are hardware used to create digital circuits which are used to represent Boolean functions. Boolean functions can only have either a "true" or "false" value. The Boolean operators needed for this exam are: AND, OR, NOT. These can be combined in logic conditions to be evaluated by the program based on the current values in the program.

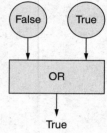

Boolean functions represented by truth tables are not on the AP exam, but are useful for understanding the Boolean logic values. They map out all possible combinations of the values to determine if a Boolean condition evaluates to true or false.

**AND** – for the "And" condition to evaluate to be true, both conditions must be true.

> **Example:** This compound condition checks to see if a person is 18 or over and is registered to vote. Both must be true to vote.
>
> IF (age ≥ 18 AND registered_to_vote = "yes")
>
> DISPLAY ("You may vote")

**OR** – only one of the conditions must be true to be true. Both can be true as well.

> **Example:**
>
> IF (battery_charge < 20% OR ride_bus_to_school)
>
> DISPLAY ("Charge your phone!")

**NOT** – changes the value to its opposite: true becomes false, false becomes true when NOT is applied.

> **Example:**
>
> IF (NOT lightning)
>
> go_swimming
> ELSE
> go_to_movies

## Truth Table Example
### T = True, F = False

| P | Q | NOT P | NOT Q | P OR Q | NOT P AND NOT Q |
|---|---|---|---|---|---|
| | | Takes the opposite value of P from column 1 | Takes the opposite value of Q from column 2 | One or both true values in column 1 and column 2 make this true | Both values in column 3 and column 4 must be true for this to be true |
| Battery charge < 20% | Ride bus to school | Battery >= 20% | Drive to school | P OR Q | NOT P AND NOT Q |
| T | T | F | F | T | F |
| T | F | F | T | T | F |
| F | T | T | F | T | F |
| F | F | T | T | F | T |

## Overflow Errors

Overflow errors occur in computers when the number to be represented is larger than the computer can hold. This varies for different computers, and you are not expected to know this value for each computer for the AP exam.

Think of it like a car odometer when it is at the highest value it can show.

When you travel one more mile or kilometer, the odometer can roll over to 000001. A computer does not roll over to 1 when it reaches the maximum value it can hold.

The overflow error for an expected positive number as the result is a negative number and the result indicating an overflow error for an expected negative number is a positive number.

**Example:** Assume 999 is the largest number that can be represented. If you add 1 to it, you would expect the result to be 1000. Since the computer cannot process this number, it produces -1000 as the result which is the smallest number our example here can represent. It does the addition, but 1 is now in the sign position, which sets our value to be negative. Your program will not produce an error when this occurs. Be sure to test for this condition, especially when you know very large or small numbers may be used with the program.

| Sign bit 1 = on | 9 | 9 | 9 |
|---|---|---|---|
| | | + | 1 |
| 1 | 0 | 0 | 0 |

## Rounding or Round-off Errors

Rounding errors occur because of the way numbers with decimal points are stored in the computer. They are imprecise and are stored as a whole number + the decimal point + the fractional part of the number. This imprecise nature can cause rounding errors and possibly inaccurate results in your programs.

**Example:** 1.0 could be stored as 0.999999998

Note that whole numbers are stored precisely as the integer they represent.

### Levels of Abstraction: High-Level Languages Versus Low-Level Languages

High-level programming languages, such as App Inventor, Python, or Java, are far more natural-language oriented than low-level languages are. Programs written in these languages can run on almost any device. They must be compiled down to the machine code level (0s and 1s) to actually execute, but the programmer does not interact with the code at that level. Therefore, many of the machine language details are abstracted or generalized away at the high-level. This makes it easier and much faster for people to write programs. These programs also run slower since they have to be compiled before executing.

```
play1 = input("What playlist would you like to hear?")
print(play1, "is an excellent choice. Here's the first song.")
```

Low-level languages are one step up from the machine language. They are also known as "assembly" languages. They are specific to a particular computer and are much more difficult to code. They do not need to be compiled, as the computer can run the code in its current form, and therefore run faster than high-level languages.

```
mov
mov
add   Sum
load  Sum
write
halt
```

# Software: Applications and Development Environments

### Variables and Constants

Variables are an abstraction for the value it holds at a time. It could be a temperature or an amount of money among countless other values. Well-named variables are helpful to programmers and those who may need to update a program much later. Remember in programming, variables can change their value through an assignment statement. It can be a simple assignment statement or through evaluating an expression.

#### Example:

outsideTemp = 50      (assignment statement)
pay = hours * rate      (expression to evaluate)

Constants, such as pi, can be stored as variables, but their value does not change. It is useful to hold the value in a well-named variable to avoid having to type in the value each time it is needed. A typo in a variable or command name would be caught as a syntax error, but an error in typing the value would be accepted by the compiler, making it much more difficult to identify the error. Constant variable names are usually written in all capital letters.

#### Examples:

PI = 3.1415
MAX_SEATS=345

### Expressions

Expressions are also abstractions because you could have a calculation to evaluate, or solve, to know the value to store in the variable. As an example, to convert from Fahrenheit to Celsius, you would have a formula, or expression, to solve to know the value.

celsiusTemp = (outsideTemp − 32) * (5 / 9)                    (expression evaluated)

### Procedures

In coding, using procedures, also called functions, to reuse code is an example of abstraction. Parameters, in particular, provide added ability to reuse the section of code multiple times with different inputs. Parameters hold the values sent in as arguments by the calling program. Each

```
define convertTemp(fahr):
    ...
    ...
    return(celsius)
```

time a procedure is called, different values can be sent to it from the calling program. This is one key feature of the abstraction and flexibility of procedures. See the chapter on algorithms for more information on procedures.

### Libraries/APIs

Libraries, also referred to as APIs (Application Programming Interface), are groups of programs already tested and combined in a library, usually of similar programs, such as a "math" library. They are available for use through importing into your program. These programs are abstractions because you can use them without knowing the details of how they work. Like procedures or functions, they can be reused by many people, and many times within one program.

**Examples:**
import math.library
randomNum = math.random(0,100)      (generate a random number between 0—100)

# The Use of Abstractions in Hardware and Software

### Hardware Abstractions

There are both low-level and high-level uses of hardware in a computer. As abstractions, these are simplified to their basic function.

- Low-level

A low-level hardware abstraction is a transistor. Transistors turn the electrical currents on and off. Recall that any electrical current level above a threshold is "on" or "1" in binary. Anything below that threshold is "off" or a "0" in binary. We do not have to know exactly how these work, just that they do work creating the basic building blocks for computers to function. Computer chips have billions of transistors on them.

- High-level

An example of a high-level hardware abstraction is the motherboard. It controls all aspects of the computer. It has multiple computer chips on it, providing it billions and billions of transistors, the low-level hardware abstraction.

## Moore's Law

Gordon Moore, the co-founder of Intel, once defined an observation that the number of transistors on integrated circuits doubled every two years. While not a law in scientific terms, this prediction applied for many years. It does not exactly apply to the same time intervals today, but computing power continues to increase exponentially.

## Hardware Architecture

The model for hardware was designed by John von Neumann, and its structure is still in use today. Computers are comprised of:

- Input
- CPU
- Control Unit
- Arithmetic/Logic Unit
- Memory
- Output

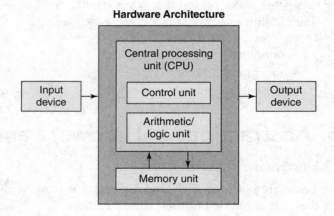

With input, we have several devices that are abstractions. Keyboards, mice, microphones, and touchscreen devices are all examples of input devices. We do not have to know how these devices take our "input" and process it to present it in a format recognizable to the program. Those details are abstracted away.

Similarly with output, we have devices such as monitors, printers, and speakers, among others, that are abstracted as output. We do not know how the program sends output in a variety of forms, such as text or music, to the devices. That is the abstraction aspect.

## Combining Low-Level Abstractions to Make New Higher-Level Abstractions

Remember in coding that we should break down our solution to the programming challenge we need to solve. Small segments of code can be written, tested, and then used over and over as needed in our program. We do not need to think about how these work anymore, only that they do work.

These low-level procedures can be combined to create any type of software solution needed. For example, procedures are used for creating email. There are functions for sending, viewing, organizing, deleting, replying, and so on that are used to solve the problem of being able to send written information to another individual for response at a time convenient for them.

Software applications are developed using hardware and software.

## Models and Simulations

Models can be used to create a simplified representation of something, such as an airplane, and then potential solutions can be simulated to see how they impact the model. This is an example of abstraction at a very high level. The model represents the real world in some way, but details are removed to focus on the impact of the solution on the model.

Hypotheses can be evaluated and then refined with the use of simulations and models. For example, scientific phenomena can be tested in the laboratory rather than having to wait for the next real-world occurrence. This reduces cost and saves time. The models and simulations can also be modified based on the results of tests and then retested. In a simulated environment, many more tests can be performed and evaluated leading to new findings, insights, and solutions.

For example, Google Earth is a model of the planet Earth, with topography, borders, roads, cities, and some buildings represented. Simulations could be used to the shortest distance to travel between two locations. Simulations could be used to test potentially dangerous situations without putting anyone at risk.

# › Review Questions

## Concepts

1. Which of the following best describes abstraction?
   - (A) Adding complexity so the concept can apply to more uses
   - (B) Simplifying complexity to make the concept more general
   - (C) Combining procedures to make a new one
   - (D) A set of instructions to do something

2. What is one way in which number systems are abstract?
   - (A) The same amount can be represented by different number representations.
   - (B) A number can only be represented by one number system.
   - (C) Symbols can be used to add, subtract, multiply, or divide them.
   - (D) They are constants.

3. What is the number system used by computers?
   - (A) Base 10 (decimal)
   - (B) Base 8 (octal)
   - (C) Base 2 (binary)
   - (D) Base 16 (hexadecimal)

4. What is $214_{10}$ in binary?
   - (A) 11010100
   - (B) 11010110
   - (C) 11010111
   - (D) 01101011

5. The letter "M" in the ASCII table is represented by 01001101 in binary. What is this in hexadecimal?
   - (A) 4E
   - (B) 413
   - (C) 4D
   - (D) 1101

6. With Boolean, what does "A AND B" mean?
   - (A) Neither A or B can be true for the condition to be true.
   - (B) If A is true, then the condition is true.
   - (C) If B is true, then the condition is true.
   - (D) Both A and B must be true for the condition to be true.

7. Which are more abstract: high-level or low-level programming languages?
   - (A) High-level
   - (B) Low-level
   - (C) Both have the same level of abstraction
   - (D) Neither are abstract

8. Which number type is stored imprecisely in memory?
   - (A) Integers
   - (B) Numbers with decimals
   - (C) Both
   - (D) Neither

9. Procedures are abstract:
   - (A) By the use of parameters
   - (B) By being easier to manage

(C) By being able to be used multiple times

(D) All of the above

**10.** What is a smaller representation of something, such as an event or process that can be used to determine what could happen in the real world?

(A) A model

(B) A plan

(C) An image

(D) A miniature

## Application of Concepts

**11.** How many more bits are available if you go from a 32-bit computer to a 64-bit machine?

(A) Twice as many

(B) 32 more

(C) $2^{32}$ more

(D) $32^2$ more

**12.** How are procedures a form of abstraction?

(A) By being able to use a procedure without knowing how it works.

(B) By understanding the code in a procedure to use it correctly.

(C) By modifying the code in a procedure for a particular use.

(D) By eliminating the use of procedures to make the code more abstract.

**13.** What order should these be in to go from smallest to largest?

1. Binary – 01110111
2. Decimal – 111
3. Hexadecimal – 9D

(A) 1, 2, 3

(B) 2, 1, 3

(C) 3, 1, 2

(D) 3, 2, 1

**14.** Which piece of hardware is the least abstract?

(A) Logic gate

(B) Transistor

(C) Circuit

(D) Processor

## › Answers and Explanations

**1. B**—Abstraction means simplifying and taking away details to make something more general and flexible.

**2. A**—Number systems are abstract because the same amount can be represented by different number representations.

**3. C**—Computers use the binary or base 2 number system consisting of 0s and 1s.

**4. B**—$214_{10}$ is 11010110 in binary.

**5. C**—$01001101_2 = 4D_{16}$

**6. D**—AND means both conditions must be true for the condition to be true.

**7. A**—High-level programming languages are more like natural language than low-level ones. The commands in the language are more general and therefore more abstract than low-level languages which are closer to machine language.

**8. B**—Integers, or whole numbers, are stored precisely. Numbers with a decimal and fractional part are stored imprecisely in computer memory.

**9. D**—The use of parameters allows a procedure to be called multiple times and apply the same code to different values. Descriptive names for procedures help identify their general function. All of these are reasons why procedures are abstract.

**10. A**—Models can be used to test events on a smaller representation to help determine the impact of the same event in real life.

**11. C**—The computer increases from $2^{32}$ to $2^{64}$ bits. Therefore, the increase is $2^{32}$ bits.

**12. A**—Procedures are abstractions because they can be used multiple times in programs with different values passed in through parameters without needing to know how they work.

**13. B**—The binary number, 01110111 converts to 119 in decimal. The hexadecimal number, 9D, converts to 157. Therefore the decimal number is smallest, then binary, then hexadecimal.

**14. B**—Transistors form circuits which form logic gates which form processors. Therefore, transistors are the least abstract since all the rest contain them as they become more abstract.

# › Rapid Review

Computers, at their lowest level, use binary numbers, 0 and 1, to represent everything. Therefore, a sequence of binary numbers could represent an object such as a number, color, sound, image, or instruction, among others. Computer programs are written to interpret the sequence based on what they need.

Numbers are an abstraction to represent "how many". Different number systems, such as decimal, binary, octal, and hexadecimal, express "how many" in different representations. These number representations can be converted to other number systems. Rounding and overflow errors can occur due to how the decimal portion of numbers are stored in computers and the maximum and minimum ranges that computers can hold, respectively.

Computer applications are developed using hardware and software. Hardware uses transistors and logic gates at its lowest level along with the motherboard, CPU, storage and input and output devices at higher levels of abstraction.

Software development can use higher-level languages, which are more abstract, or lower-level programming languages that are less abstract. Both types of programming languages use abstractions such as variables, expressions, procedures, and libraries which help make the programs more efficient and effective.

Procedures are constructs in software that allow different values to be sent to procedures via parameters. This makes procedures more flexible because they can then be used multiple times with a variety of values. The functionality the procedures provide can be combined to create new programs.

The program code is translated, (e.g., compiled or interpreted), into machine language that the computer can then run.

Models are simplified versions, and therefore abstract representations of different objects or environments. Simulations using models enable people to test hypotheses by changing the values of variables with different tests while holding others constant, running multiple tests, and doing so quickly in a safe environment.

Remember that abstractions occur when details are removed and similarities remain.

# CHAPTER 7

# Data and Information

Big Idea # 3 of the AP Computer Science Principles Course

IN THIS CHAPTER

**Summary:** This chapter focuses on how computers can be used to store, secure, and process large amounts of data and to make sense of it for either solving problems or for identifying new findings.

### Key Ideas
✪ Computers can clean, process, and classify data much better and faster than people can.
✪ Collaboration is important to identifying insights.
✪ Communicating information visually helps get the message across.
✪ Scalability is key to processing large data sets effectively and efficiently.
✪ Storage needs led to the creation of compression techniques.

---

### Key Terms

Big data
Classifying data
Cleaning data
Collaboration
Filtering data
Lossless data compression
Lossy data compression

Metadata
Patterns in data
Pixel
Privacy
Scalability
Security
Server farm

# Processing Data to Get Information

So much raw data is being collected constantly in all fields. Every purchase you make, those you return, websites you visit—all involve data that businesses collect. But what does it mean? Computers enable us to process data to turn it into information for decision making and research. Computers can often identify patterns in data that individuals would not be able to detect. As is often the case, there are also trade-offs to consider with large amounts of data.

Data collected from all types of events—including visits, searches, inquiries, orders, returns, temperatures, scores, attendees, acres planted, acres lost, acres harvested, fish, birds, photos, videos, and audio files are considered to be raw data. These are all just values and descriptions until we make sense of it. While humans can usually do an adequate job on small amounts of data, there is no way we could process the vast amounts of data now collected in many raw data sets. We get tired, distracted, and bored, and then errors occur or opportunities are missed.

## How Computers Help Process Data

- **Cleaning:** One area computers are very helpful with is "cleaning" the data. This includes removing corrupt data, removing or repairing incomplete data, and verifying ranges or dates among other steps. Removing or flagging invalid data is very useful. Again, individuals could easily miss errors in the data, which could cause incorrect results in later processing.
- **Filtering:** Computers are also able to easily "filter" data. This means different subsets can be identified and extracted to help people make meaning of the data. For example, all temperature values greater than 98.6 could be meaningful and need further processing or perhaps just a count of how many there are in the entire data set.
- **Classifying:** Additionally, computers can help make meaning of large data sets by grouping data with common features and values. These groupings or classifications would be based on criteria provided by people who need to work with the data. There could be single or multiple criteria used for these groupings. It would depend on the reason that the data was collected.
- **Patterns:** Computers are able to identify patterns in data that people are either unable to recognize or cannot process enough data to see the pattern. This process is known as "data mining." New discoveries and understandings are often made this way. When new or unexpected patterns emerge, the data has been transformed into information for people to begin to interpret. Computers make processing huge amounts of data possible so people can make sense of it.

Machine learning is related to data mining, but it uses the data to make predictions. Through these predictions, actions can be programmed to occur when certain criteria are met, making it appear the device has "learned" how to react or perform.

## How People Work with Computers to Process Data

- **Collaboration:** Collaboration is a technique especially useful in working to analyze data. Having a group with different backgrounds, specialties, cultures, and perspectives can result in better analysis and use of the data. Someone may ask or notice something that others with similar backgrounds or someone working alone would not. This could lead to a new hypothesis or discovery about what the data represents.

The use of technology now makes collaboration much easier. Remember that the Web was created to allow scientists across the globe to share documents for collaboration. The tools are continually improving, allowing people in different time zones and locations to easily work together. Collaboration in a face-to-face environment is always beneficial, but technology provides the opportunity for many to collaborate via live-streaming and video-conferencing tools. It also provides a way for multiple people to work together on a shared document or presentation, but in their own time zone and on their own schedule.

- **Sharing and Communicating Information:** There are many tools available to aid in communicating to others the insights identified from the data. Graphics in the form of charts, tables, and other designs are useful to present data in a visual format and in summary format. Remember the phrase, "A picture paints a thousand words"? Use it. The human brain is wired to process information visually, so the use of images and other visual tools are effective ways to get a message across to help others understand it. Providing ways for others to interact with the data, such as providing sound files or videos when someone selects an option is also useful.

# Computers and Data

## Large Data Sets ("Big Data")

"Big data" does not mean large numbers, but instead means vast amounts of data. These data sets have so many records, they are too large to fit into the available memory of our computers or even servers at our locations. These files need multiple servers to hold and process the data. This has led to the creation of "server farms," which are many large computers located in one place for the purpose of processing data. Businesses, universities, governments, and even individuals can contract for these server farms to run their data through programs to do the cleaning and filtering listed above, and to then process the data looking

for the patterns, trends, and solutions. Many companies offer services including platforms for data storage and processing.

Software tools such as spreadsheets and databases are used to filter, organize, and search the data. Search tools and filtering systems are needed to help analyze the data and recognize patterns. You are not required to know details about a specific tool.

To process these extremely large data files, new methods had to be created. One, called Map Reduce, was created by Google. Hadoop is an open source version of the same processing model. The data sets are distributed over many servers. Each server processes the section of the data set it has. All servers are running the same program at the same time, and these individual solutions are then aggregated or combined for the final solution.

## Metadata

Metadata is data that describes data and can help others find data and use it more effectively. It is not the content of the data, but includes information such as:

- Date
- Time stamp
- Author/owner
- File size
- File type

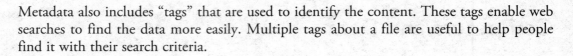

Metadata also includes "tags" that are used to identify the content. These tags enable web searches to find the data more easily. Multiple tags about a file are useful to help people find it with their search criteria.

## Scalability

Scalability is the ability to increase the capacity of a resource without having to go to a completely new solution, and for that resource to continue to operate at acceptable levels. The increase should be transparent to the users of the resource. For example, processing should not slow down as the amount of data increases when solutions are scalable. In the case of data, the resource would be additional servers to store and process the data. Scalability is an important aspect to be able to store and process large data sets. These files cannot fit on our computers or most organizations' servers. The tools we can use to process them change as the file size grows.

The "cloud" is considered a scalable resource. People connect, store, share, and communicate across the Internet. As traffic or demand for resources increases, the cloud service manages the demand by providing additional resources such as servers.

Networks can also provide scalability. As more devices are added to the network, network managers increase access points and other devices to accommodate the additional network devices and traffic.

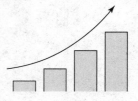

Note that scalability also includes the ability to downsize as needed, again without impacting the storage or processing.

# Concerns Regarding Data and Information

## Security

The security of our data deals with the ability to prevent unauthorized individuals from gaining access to it and preventing those who can view our data from changing it. Strong passwords help block those trying to gain unauthorized access. That is one reason many sites have increased their password requirements to contain components such as:

- Must contain a capital letter
- Must contain a number
- Must contain a special character
- Must be a specified minimum length
- Cannot be the same or almost the same as a previous password
- Cannot be the same as the user ID

Good security for those who need access to certain features of a program include only providing "read" access to those who should not change anything. Very few people would then have "update" and "delete" access limiting accidental or deliberate changes.

We trust the companies that maintain our personal information, including social security number and financial information, like credit card numbers, to keep it secure. As the news often reports, many companies have had their security defenses breached and customer data stolen. The data often is sold to those planning to use unsuspecting users' identities to open accounts and make purchases. Always check your accounts often!

Security also relates to encrypting data before it is transmitted to ensure it remains secure if it is intercepted during transmission. The receiving location would decrypt the data for it to then be used as needed.

# Privacy

Digital footprints and fingerprints are the trail of little pieces of data we leave behind as a sign of our presence as we go through our daily life. Some of the ways our data is collected occurs via:

- GPS coordinates embedded in photographs and apps showing our location
- Financial transactions such as viewing, comparing, and making purchases
- Websites visited
- Cell phones pinging off towers
- Key card access to locations

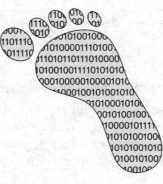

Many people willingly provide personal information to sites to gain access or privileges whether it's through sports teams, shopping, or restaurants. Their data is stored and may be sold with or without their knowledge.

Some sites claim to aggregate data to protect individual privacy. This means summarizing, removing some aspects, and masking the data findings at such a high level that no individual or group should be identified. However, done incorrectly, individual information can and has been identifiable. It is surprising how one small identifiable piece of data, such as a zip code, can be used with other legally available public sources of data on the Web to identify a person. All too often, this invasion of privacy is either posted or shared in ways unknown to those impacted.

# Storing Data

### Representing Digital Data

New names for numbers have been created to account for these large amounts of data. These have been identified and agreed upon by the members of the International System of Units (SI). While the American and European number systems are different, all countries agree with SI number identifiers.

- Remember that a bit, "binary digit," is the smallest unit for computers and is either 0 or 1.
- A byte is made up of 8 bits. It is the basic unit used to describe memory.
- A kilobyte is approximately 1,000 ("kilo") bytes.
- A megabyte is approximately 1,000,000 bytes (or a thousand kilobytes).

Note the powers of 10 and 2 in the table below.

| SI Naming Convention | Power in Binary | Power in Decimal | American Naming Convention |
|---|---|---|---|
| Kilo | $2^{10}$ | $10^3$ | Thousand |
| Mega | $2^{20}$ | $10^6$ | Million |
| Giga | $2^{30}$ | $10^9$ | Billion |
| Tera | $2^{40}$ | $10^{12}$ | Trillion |
| Peta | $2^{50}$ | $10^{15}$ | Quadrillion |
| Exa | $2^{60}$ | $10^{18}$ | Quintillion |
| Zetta | $2^{70}$ | $10^{21}$ | Sextillion |
| Yotta | $2^{80}$ | $10^{24}$ | Septillion |

You do not have to know these number systems for the AP exam.

There are considerations that have to be constantly evaluated when it comes to storing data.

### Data Compression: Lossless and Lossy

There are also trade-offs for storing data. Image files become large very quickly. Therefore, compression techniques were developed to decrease their size. Raster or Bitmap images store data by pixel (picture element). If you had an image that was 300 × 400 pixels = 120,000 pixels, and with 3 bytes per pixel, it would take approximately 120000 * 3 = 360,000 bytes for one picture. A 10-MB pixel image would take 30,000,000 bytes, or 240,000,000 bits. Depending on the bandwidth, this image could take 30 to 60 seconds to download, which is quite slow for one image. Vector graphics have smaller file sizes than raster images.

We can reduce the amount of space needed through **data compression:**

- **Lossless** compression techniques allow the original image to be restored. No data is lost, but the file size cannot be as compressed as with lossy techniques.
- **Lossy** compression techniques lose some data in the compression process. The original can never be restored, but the compression is greater than with lossless techniques.

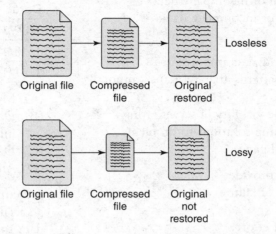

JPEG (Joint Photographic Experts Group) images reduce file sizes up to 90% by replacing similar colors with the same color as large parts of the image. The replacements generally cannot be detected by the human eye.

Note that the same concepts apply for music and video files. There are lossy and lossless compression programs that can be used with these files. As with image files, the original file can be restored with the lossless technique, but not with a lossy one.

Many compression techniques assign a code to each character, including numbers and special characters. Characters that appear more frequently get a shorter code; those that appear less frequently get a longer code. The larger the file, the greater the opportunity for a larger savings on file size. For example, bitmap images are files that are usually quite large.

The format the data is stored in plays a role. The two to three-character file extension is used to determine what software tools can open and process the data.

Note too that more storage space will be needed to process files that need to be updated or "written to" versus simply read. This is because a copy of the file will be made for writing to it, in part to keep a backup copy in case it needs to be restored, as well as to handle the space needs of modifying the file. Opening files for read only access does not require this extra space.

## › Review Questions

### Concepts

1. Why is cleaning data important?
   (A) It ensures incomplete data does not hide or skew results.
   (B) It removes bad or incomplete data.
   (C) It repairs bad or incomplete data.
   (D) All the above

2. Why is analyzing big data important?
   (A) To identify patterns that humans cannot see
   (B) To increase the viability of server farms
   (C) To verify existing solutions to problems
   (D) To test due diligence

3. Collaboration can provide
   (A) several points of failure
   (B) clean data
   (C) duplication of effort
   (D) insights we may never discover otherwise

4. Information about the author of a document is
   (A) metadata
   (B) content
   (C) context
   (D) maxdata

5. Being able to add or remove resources to store large data sets is called
   (A) scalability
   (B) filtering
   (C) efficiency
   (D) routing

6. Providing someone read-only access to data is an example of
   (A) security
   (B) privacy
   (C) encryption
   (D) ciphering

7. Which data compression technique provides the most compression?
   (A) Lossy
   (B) Lossless
   (C) Filtering
   (D) Classification

### Application of Concepts

8. Given a table of lunchroom leftovers, what can be determined from the data?

| Date | Total Meals | Total Meals Leftover |
|---|---|---|
| 1/29/18 | 800 | 25 |
| 1/30/18 | 750 | 5 |
| 1/31/18 | 800 | 42 |

   (A) Most popular items
   (B) Days of field trips when classes missed lunch
   (C) Days with high absenteeism
   (D) Amount of wasted budget dollars

9. A company purchases a large block of data from a social media site. If they want to analyze the data to learn more about potential customers, what techniques should they use?
   (A) Modeling to test different hypotheses about what data could be present
   (B) Data mining to identify patterns and relationships in the data for further analysis
   (C) Maximization to get the highest return on their purchase of the data
   (D) Data processing to use the data with existing company software to see if it will run on their systems or if new ones will need to be developed

10. A magnet school wants to advertise their students' success taking AP exams to prospective families. What's the best method to share the summarized data?
    (A) Post an image of student results on social media sites.
    (B) Create an interactive pie chart that can drill down to topics and overall scores posted on the school's website.
    (C) Write a report for a marketing pamphlet.
    (D) Send an email to families with middle-school-age children.

11. Which topic needs data mining to resolve?
    (A) The average number of students who drive to school each day
    (B) The record of wins and losses for all sports teams under their current coaches compared to prior years' win/loss records
    (C) The number of library books that need to be replaced each year
    (D) The standardized test scores for current students compared to all other test scores across the country for the past decade

## › Answers and Explanations

1. **D**—Data needs to be cleaned to remove or repair corrupt or incomplete data to ensure valid data is used for research and analysis.

2. **A**—Analyzing big data allows us to identify patterns that could help solve problems or identify new possibilities that people likely could not process.

3. **D**—Collaboration can provide the possibility of insights we may never get otherwise by having team members with different backgrounds and perspectives create, design, and evaluate data, documents, products, etc.

4. **A**—Information about the author of a document is metadata.

5. **A**—Scalability is adding or removing resources to store and process large data sets.

6. **A**—Security is providing the appropriate level of access to data or software functionality.

7. **A**—Lossy data compression provides the most compression.

8. **D**—While answers B and C hint at the cause, you cannot tell for sure from the table data. You can take the number of meals left over and multiply it by the cost of each meal to determine the budget dollars lost.

9. **B**—Data mining is the analysis of data to identify patterns and connections. Companies can then use the data to identify business opportunities to take advantage of or threats to avoid.

10. **B**—Prospective families will likely check the school's website for additional information. Therefore, an interactive pie chart can provide high-level information and drill down to more information when sections of the pie are selected. Social media accounts may not reach all families, and a marketing pamphlet cannot provide as much information or the drill down ability. Sending a mass email may be flagged as spam and families may not open an email from an unknown source.

11. **D**—The test scores compared to all other scores for the prior decade will be a large data set. Searching for correlations between current student data and prior data is a data-mining task. The other options will have exact numbers on manageable-sized data sets that a person could identify manually or by using a local computer for processing.

# ❯ Rapid Review

Data is being generated all the time, all around us, by sensors, mouse clicks, camera clicks, recordings, buttons pressed, and swipes among many other ways. This data can provide valuable information to various interested parties but only once it has been processed by computers. Then, the data can be analyzed to see what new information can be extracted.

Processing raw data includes activities such as cleaning and filtering data. It can also include classifying the data into various groupings. These activities may help identify patterns in the data that can then provide valuable information. A concern with processing data is ensuring the privacy of anyone whose information is included.

Collaborating with others who have different backgrounds and experiences should produce better hypotheses and better analysis of the results. Such collaborations are also more likely to identify insights that an individual working alone would not spot. If face-to-face meetings are not possible, there are many online collaboration tools that can help when those working together are in different locations and time zones.

Once data has been processed and analyzed into information, it needs to be communicated to other interested groups. Visual representations can effectively communicate the findings and can be done through tables, diagrams, charts, summary representations, or interactive displays.

Metadata is identifying data about data, such as date and time created and owner of the data or computer artifact. It is important because when metadata is used effectively, searches for and of data can more effectively find what the person needs.

"Big data" means data sets that are so large, humans cannot process them manually. Computers must be used to help find the patterns, trends, and connections the data provide. There are tools, such as spreadsheets and databases, to store the data and then run queries to identify features of the data. Big data is too large to use standard processing tools and needs scalable solutions such as server farms that can seamlessly add more resources as the data grows to store and process it.

Transmitting the data to and from locations creates a security concern to ensure the data is not intercepted or corrupted while in transit. Concerns also exist around how to send such large amounts of data. Compression techniques, both lossy and lossless, were created and use algorithms to decrease the original file size to make transmission and storage easier. Lossless techniques enable the original file to be restored while lossy techniques create smaller files, but the original file cannot be restored.

# Algorithms

Big Idea # 4 of the AP Computer Science Principles Course

**IN THIS CHAPTER**

**Summary:** Algorithms are solutions designed to solve problems. Algorithms are fundamental to programming.

**Key Ideas**

- ✪ Algorithms are instructions to complete any type of task, from cooking to coding.
- ✪ Algorithms can be written using sequential, selection, and repetitive statements.
- ✪ Intractable algorithms cannot run in a reasonable amount of time; they are usually for large data sets.
- ✪ Undecidable problems have no solution for all instances.
- ✪ Heuristics can sometimes be used to find a solution that is close enough.
- ✪ Algorithms can be analyzed for clarity, correctness, and efficiency.

---

**Key Terms**

Algorithm

Binary search

Boolean values

Clarity

Condition

Correctness

Efficiency

Heuristic

Intractable

Iterative

Linear search
Logical operators
Readability

Selection
Sequential
Undecidable

# Algorithms: The Basics

An algorithm is a set of steps to do a task. Recipes are algorithms. They are a set of steps to prepare food. Instructions for taking medicine make up an algorithm. Directions to get from location "x" to location "y" are an algorithm.

In Computer Science, algorithms are the set of steps to solve a problem. Algorithms are implemented with software. Examples are programs to:

- Calculate grade averages
- Run the air conditioner when the room temperature reaches 78°F
- Calculate the shortest route from home to school on your GPS

## Three Types of Program Statements

A combination of three types of programming statements can be used to create algorithms to solve a computational problem.

- **Sequential**
  These are statements that are executed as written in the program. Once a statement is complete, the next statement is run.
- **Selection**
  These are "if" statements and are a key component to many programs. They use the "if (condition)" construct and the evaluation of the condition uses Boolean values. These can only be either true or false so the program statements associated with the condition only run when the condition at that moment evaluates to "true".

```
IF grade_point_average ≥ 90
      grade ← "A"
```

- **Iterative**
  Iterative statements, also called "loops," are run over and over until the condition associated with it evaluates to be false. Each iteration through the loop must change the condition; otherwise, you have an infinite loop. An infinite loop is one that will never end and only stops when all the resources on the computer it is running on are used up. You can also have a loop within a loop.

  You are responsible for understanding the "REPEAT n TIMES" and "REPEAT UNTIL (condition)" loops for the AP exam.

  REPEAT n TIMES Loop

  This loop will repeat a specified number of times; "n" is a variable that must be set to a positive integer for the loop to run.

```
num = 5
REPEAT num TIMES
    ...
```

  REPEAT UNTIL (condition) loop

  The REPEAT UNTIL loop has a condition to evaluate at each iteration of the loop.

The loop will continue to run while the condition evaluates to "false". As with the REPEAT n TIMES loop, the value tested in the condition must change to avoid an infinite loop. This is similar to how an "if" statement works. However, remember that "if" statements execute once. REPEAT UNTIL loops can execute multiple times or not at all, depending on how the condition evaluates.

```
REPEAT UNTIL (num > 5)
    …
```

## Boolean Values and Expressions

Boolean values can only be true or false. Expressions using Booleans can only evaluate to either true or false. Relational operators are used with Boolean values. These are:

| | |
|---|---|
| = | equal |
| ≠ | not equal |
| > | greater than |
| < | less than |
| ≥ | greater than or equal to |
| ≤ | less than or equal to |

Two values are compared based on the logic operator and determined to be true or false. For example:

$x = 5$
$y = 10$
$x > y$ evaluates to false because at this moment, x is 5 and y is 10

Boolean values are used with IF statements and REPEAT UNTIL loops. As long as the condition evaluates to be true, the code with the IF statement will be executed. The REPEAT UNTIL (condition) runs "until" the condition becomes true.

## Compound Conditional Statements (AND, OR, NOT)

The conditions can be simple or compound. Multiple conditions can be combined using the logical operators: AND, OR, and NOT.
- To be true, both of the conditions on either side of the AND operator must be true when evaluated individually.
- For the OR condition, either or both of the conditions can be true for the condition to be true.
- With the NOT operator, if a condition was true, then NOT makes it false. If a condition was false, then NOT makes it true.

## Else Statement

Each IF statement can also have an ELSE statement. The ELSE is optional, but it must have an IF statement. The statements associated with the ELSE will only run when the IF condition is "false".

```
lightning ← true
IF (NOT lightning)
      swimming ← "yes"
ELSE
      movie ← "yes"
```

Just as with IF statements, conditions for loops can be combined using the Boolean operators AND, OR, and NOT.

In your Create project, you may have had ELSE IF statements. These will not be tested on the multiple-choice questions on the AP exam.

Remember that these will be on the Exam Reference Sheet you will have during the multiple-choice exam.

# Using Algorithms

### Combining Algorithms

One of the key features of algorithms is that you can use them over and over, and combine them for more complex problem solving.

For example, you can create an algorithm to ask a user to select a menu option by typing in the number.

- To ensure the user typed in a valid number, you could call a different algorithm to check for a valid number.
- If the number is not valid, call a third algorithm to display an error message.
- If the number is valid, call the algorithm to process the selected option.

Each of these algorithms can work in a variety of difference scenarios. By creating them and ensuring they are accurate, using them in a new algorithm saves time and helps ensure the new algorithm produces accurate results.

There are also libraries associated with different programming languages. These libraries consist of program solutions for algorithms that can be imported and used in programs. Use of these can also save time and help ensure correct results in the new algorithm.

However, be aware that there is more than one correct algorithm to create a solution for a problem at hand. Finding different algorithmic solutions can be helpful in identifying new insights about the problem. Different algorithms may also have different levels of efficiency or clarity.

### Languages for Algorithms

Algorithms can be written in several ways. Natural language is our native speaking and writing language, so it is much easier for people to use and understand.

Programming languages are very strict with their syntax, which is like their grammar and structure. This includes both block style programming languages and textual programming languages. These are written for the computer to execute and may be more difficult for beginning programmers to understand. Pseudocode is a combination of natural and programming languages. As you first start out designing algorithms, you will likely use more natural language features. As you learn more about a programming language, your pseudocode may begin to include more coding-like features. Pseudocode cannot run on computers and needs to be translated to a programming language to do so. While most programming languages are fairly equitable in being able to implement an algorithm in the code, some were written for specific uses in a particular subject area, such as physics, and are better suited for these uses.

# The Limits of Algorithms

### Intractable Problems

Algorithms have limits, and there are some problems for which we do not have efficient enough algorithms to solve. These are called "intractable" problems. As the data set grows large, the algorithm is too inefficient to process the data. The algorithm could work for smaller data sets but needs exponential time or resources to run for large amounts of data. This can be good, as intractability is an aspect of cryptography that keeps our personal information private. There are too many options to check each one. However, the day may come when these problems can be solved as advances continue to be made in computers.

Often, intractable problems can use a "heuristic" approach. This is an approach that may not be optimal, but is close enough to use as a solution. One common example is the Traveling Salesman problem. Given a list of cities, find the shortest path between them all. The algorithm to make a list of every possible path and then choose the shortest one becomes unwieldly very quickly. The heuristic approach is to find the nearest neighbor to a city and take that path. Then find the nearest neighbor to that city and so on. This modified algorithm is achievable in a reasonable amount of time and resource usage, so it is a viable solution.

**NOTE:** You will *not* have to find heuristic solutions on the AP exam.

### Undecidable/Unsolvable Problems

These are problems that cannot be solved. There is no algorithm that can solve all cases of the problem. A decidable problem is one where an algorithm can be written that results in a "yes" or "no" answer for all inputs. Determining if a number is prime is an example of a decidable problem.

In contrast, an undecidable problem does not have an algorithm that can give a correct "yes" or "no" for each instance. The Halting Problem is one example of an unsolvable problem. It states that "given an arbitrary computer program, with an arbitrary input, decide whether it has an infinite loop."

**NOTE:** You will *not* have to determine whether a problem is undecidable on the AP exam.

# Analyzing Algorithms

### Algorithm Correctness

An algorithm's correctness refers to its accuracy and whether or not it contains errors. It is determined by mathematical reasoning rather than by testing. More than one correct algorithm can be created to solve a task.

**NOTE:** You will *not* have to prove program correctness on the AP exam.

### Algorithm Readability and Clarity

An important feature of any algorithm and program is how easy it is to read and follow. Hand-in-hand with readability is clarity. Clarity refers to how easy it is to understand. Generally, a program that is readable is clear. Readability is important to help programmers understand a program. The original programmer may not be the person who makes changes to it. Even if it is the original author, if a period of time exists between writing it and modifying it, readability and clarity will impact the time and ability of the programmer to modify or correct the code. Features of readability and clarity include variables and procedures that are named according to their use and effective documentation of the program with comments in the code.

## Algorithm Efficiency

The efficiency of algorithms deals with how long it will take to run and how much memory will be needed. This becomes especially important with extremely large data sets. While the time will vary based on the computer used, general rules are used to determine the efficiency of these algorithms.

**NOTE:** You will *not* be asked about the formal analysis (Big-O) of algorithms on the AP exam.

Efficiency can be determined by mathematically proving it and actually running it on data sets of different sizes and measuring how long it took and memory resources needed.

We have talked about how there can be more than one right solution to a problem in computer science. These different solutions may all be correct and readable, but could have different efficiencies. Sometimes, more complex algorithms can be more efficient, and more efficient algorithms may be able to better handle larger data sets.

## Searching

Searching deals with finding the needed data from everything in the data set. There are several common algorithms that have been written to search for items in a data set.

- Linear searches, also called sequential searches, check each individual record, one after the other in order to either find the desired data or to determine it is not in the data set. Such a search is easy to understand and simple to implement, and it does not matter if the data is sorted. With a linear search, the best case is if the item is first in the list; the worst case is if it is not in the list at all.
- Binary searches are far more efficient than linear searches. However, data must be **sorted** to use a binary search. The binary search is considered a "divide-and-conquer" algorithm because it divides the data set into two equal parts. Feedback about whether the value in question is higher or lower than the midpoint of the list determines which half to discard, and which half to continue searching. The dividing and searching steps are repeated until the value is found or determined that it is not in the list.

**NOTE:** You will not have to analyze algorithms on the AP exam.

# 〉 Review Questions

## Concepts

1. What term describes values that can only be either true or false?
   (A) Intractable
   (B) Algorithmic
   (C) Boolean
   (D) Sequential

2. What is/are used to determine whether code should be run for both "IF" statements and "REPEAT UNTIL" loops?
   (A) Pseudocode
   (B) Correctness
   (C) Conditions
   (D) Events

3. Which combination of statements can be used to express algorithms?
   (A) Iterative, sequential, and selection
   (B) Correctness, efficiency, and clarity
   (C) Readable, iterative, and efficient
   (D) Selection, conditional, and Boolean

4. What type of problem cannot currently be determined or explained by an algorithm?
   (A) Indefinite problem
   (B) Unsolvable problem
   (C) Tractable problem
   (D) Intractable problem

5. When is a compound condition using the logical operator AND true?
   (A) When either of the conditions are true
   (B) When both conditions are false
   (C) When both conditions are true
   (D) When the NOT operator is also used

6. Which type of loop runs a set number of times?
   (A) Indefinite
   (B) Repeat until
   (C) Infinite
   (D) Repeat "n" times

7. Why is a "divide-and-conquer" search more efficient than a linear search?
   (A) You only look at half the data set.
   (B) You eliminate half the data set with each iteration.
   (C) You have to search all the values.
   (D) It is less efficient with large data sets.

8. Sequential statements
   (A) run one after the other in the order given
   (B) run only when the condition is true
   (C) run until a loop finishes
   (D) run until the user enters "done"

9. Else statements
   (A) run each time an "if" condition is true
   (B) run when an "if" condition is false.
   (C) run every time an "if" statement runs
   (D) do not need an "if" statement to run

10. With a problem that cannot be solved for all cases, what can sometimes be used as a close approximation?
    (A) A travelling solution
    (B) A solvable solution
    (C) A heuristic solution
    (D) An intractable solution

## Application of Concepts

11. What is the output of the algorithm written in pseudocode below at 7:00 a.m. Friday?

```
If Monday - Friday at 8:00 a.m.
     Set thermostat to 62
If Saturday or Sunday
     Set thermostat to 70
If time is 5:00 p.m.
     Set thermostat to 68
```

    (A) 62
    (B) 68
    (C) 70
    (D) Unknown

**12.** The algorithm below is not working correctly. Which line of code will make it work as intended?

```
(Compare cars to available parking
spots)
availSlots ← 180
parkingLot ← [ ]
REPEAT UNTIL (availSlots = 0)
{
   availSlots ← availSlots - 1
}
DISPLAY (parkingLot)
```

(A)  APPEND (parkingLot, availSlot)

(B)  REMOVE(parkingLot, availSlot)

(C)  INSERT(parkingLot, availSlot, name)

(D)  REPEAT UNTIL (LENGTH(parkingLot) = LENGTH(availSlots))

**13.** Which line of code can be placed inside the braces { } to fix the following loop so it will not be an infinite loop?

```
name ← " "
REPEAT UNTIL (name = "done")
{
   DISPLAY ("Student name is: ", name)
}
```

(A)  IF name ≠ "done")

(B)  count = count + 1

(C)  name ← INPUT( )

(D)  name ← studentRoster

**14.** Below is a flowchart of an alarm clock snooze process. What value does the variable "count" have after tracing through the flowchart?

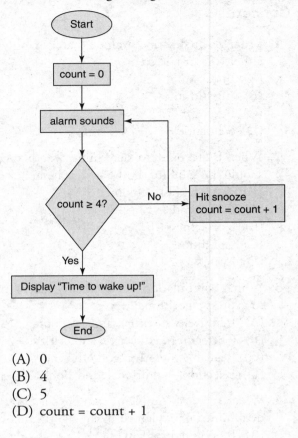

(A)  0

(B)  4

(C)  5

(D)  count = count + 1

# › Answers and Explanations

**1. C**—Boolean values can only be either true or false.

**2. C**—Conditions can be used to determine whether code should be run for both "if" statements or "repeat until" loops.

**3. A**—Algorithms can be expressed using a combination of iterative, sequential, and selection statements.

**4. B**—Problems that cannot currently be solved by an algorithm are called unsolvable.

**5. C**—A compound condition using the logical operator AND is true when both conditions are true.

**6. D**—A "REPEAT "n" TIMES" loop will run "n" times.

**7. B**—A "divide-and-conquer" search is more efficient than a linear search because you eliminate half of the data set with each iteration.

**8. A**—Sequential statements run one after the other in the order given.

**9. B**—Else statements run when an "if" condition is false.

**10. C**—A heuristic solution can be used with a problem that cannot be solved for all cases.

11. **B**—The temperature on Friday morning at 7:00 a.m. will still be 68 degrees from the third "IF" statement, which set it to 68 degrees at 5:00 p.m. the night before.

12. **A**—The list, parkingLot, starts out empty. If elements are not placed into the list, then the DISPLAY statement at the end will show an empty list. Either APPEND or INSERT can be used to add elements to a list. However, we do not have the "name" of the person assigned to a parking place, so answer A, to APPEND the number of the available parking slots to the list is the best answer.

13. **C**—The variable name is initialized to be an empty text field. This is the variable that is tested in the REPEAT UNTIL condition. An infinite loop will occur unless a way is provided to update the "name" field. The INPUT() command allows the user to enter student names and the value "done" into the "name" variable.

14. **B**—The condition to keep hitting the snooze button tests to see if count is greater than or equal to 4. After count equals 4, the flowchart processing continues to the message that it's time to wake up without increasing "count". Therefore, count equals 4 and B is the correct answer.

## › Rapid Review

Algorithms are a set of steps to complete a task. All algorithms can be written using a combination of sequential, selection, and iterative statements. Algorithms can be combined to create a new algorithm. An example is an algorithm to play a video along with the algorithms to provide features to speed it up, slow it down, mute the sound, or display the captions.

Algorithms can be written in natural language, which is our speaking language; pseudocode, which is a combination of natural language and a programming language; and both block and text-based programming languages. The natural language and pseudocode algorithms can be understood more easily than those written in a programming language. Features to make algorithms more readable and clear include adding comments and using well-named variables and procedures.

Undecidable problems are those that no algorithm can solve for all instances of the problem. There may be solutions for some cases, but not all of them. Intractable problems cannot be solved in a reasonable amount of time or with a reasonable amount of resources. As the data set gets larger, the amount of time and/or memory required becomes too large and is beyond our current capabilities to process. Heuristic approaches can often find solutions that are good enough for the need at hand.

Algorithms can be evaluated for their correctness, clarity, and efficiency. There can be more than one correct algorithm to solve a problem, and different solutions can be more efficient with different size data sets. Remember that efficiency includes memory and processing time. There can be trade-offs among different solutions as more efficient solutions may be more complex but less clear.

Binary searches use a "divide-and-conquer" technique and can only be used with sorted data sets. Linear searches check every record to either find the item in question or determine that it is not in the data set. Linear searches can be used with sorted or unsorted data sets.

# CHAPTER 9

# Programming

Big Idea # 5 of the AP Computer Science Principles Course

IN THIS CHAPTER

**Summary:** Programs implement algorithms and can be developed for any reason, personal or professional; can include all types of output; and can be shared easily. There are processes in place to create well-developed and tested programs, and abstraction can be used to manage complexity and make programs more flexible. Collaboration and iteration are key aspects of software development.

This course does not require students to use a particular programming language. Therefore, the format of questions on the exam will use a standard format found in the Exam Reference Sheet (see the Appendix). It does not follow a particular programming language and there are some key differences from most programming languages. One difference is that lists start at index position 1, which is different than many programming languages. Students must be familiar with this format to ensure they are not slowed down or confused when reading the exam questions!

Students will have a copy of the Exam Reference Sheet (see the Appendix), during the exam.

**Key Ideas**

✪ The software development process is an iterative one.

✪ Programmers work collaboratively with users and other program team members to develop and test code.

✪ Variables hold values in programs.

✪ Procedures are reusable blocks of code.

✪ Parameters in procedures accept values that can differ each time the procedure is called.

✪ Return statements send back values from a procedure to the calling program.

✪ Lists are collections used with FOR EACH loops to process each item in a list.

✪ Debugging involves finding and fixing errors in a program.

---

**Key Terms**

| | |
|---|---|
| API | Library |
| Argument | Lists |
| Assignment statement | Logical operators |
| Boolean | Parameter |
| Collaboration | Procedure |
| Debugging | SDLC |
| Floating point number | String |
| Index | Variable |
| Integers | |

# Programming and Our Lives

Computers run the world! Or so it seems, more and more. Therefore, we should all have an idea of what programming is about. Computer programs can be written for a multitude of reasons, such as for businesses, scientific research, the entertainment industry, and personal use. Programs can include video, audio, images, buttons to push, and items to drag and swipe.

Thanks to the Internet and the ease of collaboration and sharing, programs and apps (software applications) can be quickly and easily shared with people worldwide. These can sometimes have a huge impact, positive or negative, on people, and sometimes have additional results not originally foreseen by the software developer(s). Advances in programming languages, the ease of sharing with a global audience, and the ability to collaborate have spread software development to many other disciplines, such as science and art, resulting in innovation in those fields.

# The Process of Software Development

### Software Development Process—Iteration Rules!

Projects are all around us, whether it's a research paper for school, completing a science lab, producing a graduation ceremony, or planning a celebration. Computer Science also has projects in which teams or individuals write code to create solutions for their user or customer.

There is a well-defined process for running successful technology projects, the software development life cycle (SDLC). The engineering design process is similar. The process is iterative, meaning the steps are repeated and each iteration produces a better result. These are repeated several times throughout the project as new information is gathered or clarified, testing is completed and revisions are needed, or the customer changes their mind about what they need mid-project. The cycles will usually be shorter each iteration. The following steps are considered the key steps for successful project management:

**Initiate:** Kick off the project and identify team members

**Plan:** This step involves defining the problem the project needs to solve. All users with a stake in the program solution must be interviewed to document and understand what they need the project to do. Ongoing communication with the users is important to creating a successful programming solution. This stage involves understanding the problem and identifying the root cause of it and any risks or uncertainties involved with it. You will have a much better product if you thoroughly understand the problem that needs to be solved before beginning to write the code.

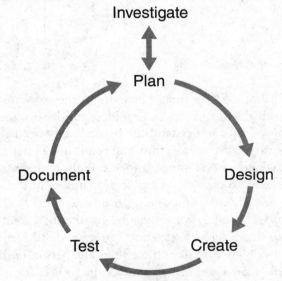

Software Development Process

**Design:** This is the step to identify how the problem can be solved. Designing, creating, and testing smaller programming modules that can be reused and combined can help create a successful programming solution. This also includes identifying and documenting assumptions and concerns from any project team member that could impact the solution. Users must be a part of this process to ensure all features needed are identified and a solution designed.

**Create:** This means creating/programming the solution from the Design phase. Breaking a project into separate programming components is a useful approach. Each component can be developed and tested, and then added to the overall project when complete. This approach works with small and large programming projects. Program modules can be added one at a time and tested to ensure the overall project still successfully works. Then an additional module can be added and tested.

**Test:** All features, using expected data and unexpected data, should be tested to determine if the programs work and if they provide the functionality as intended.

**Document:** Ideally, documentation will be created as the program is being developed. Documentation of what a program is intended to do along with documenting complex or confusing sections of code is important in coding. Well-named variables and procedures can be somewhat "self-documenting" by describing their purpose, but they do not completely take the place of additional documentation. This is so useful when you either return later to modify the code or a team member has to pick up your code and understand what it is doing to successfully make modifications.

## Collaboration

Professional programmers seldom work in isolation. Teams of people with different and similar skill sets are formed to complete the project. Collaboration among the team members and with their customers is instrumental to creating a quality solution.

Collaboration has many benefits in the software development world. From the start, by working with project stakeholders to identify the project's purpose, and closely working with users to understand the functionality needed in the project, collaborative efforts consistently prove to save time and result in a better outcome by providing differing views and ideas in the development process. It always helps to have more than one person listening to the users to provide a clear understanding of the issues to solve.

Communication among team members is crucial as they program separate modules that will need to work together for the total solution. It also helps to have someone other than the developer test the program code to identify problems and help find solutions. It is always good to have more than one person understand the problem and solutions in the event a key team member leaves the project team before it is finished.

## Debugging

Debugging involves finding and correcting errors in your program. There are steps you can take when creating your code to help with later troubleshooting:

- One of these is to use procedures rather than duplicating code. It is much easier to read and understand a shorter program and one that uses a procedure to perform the same functionality.
- Another step is to use well-named variables and procedures. If they are descriptive names that describe what they do, it is easier to trace through a program and understand what it is supposed to do.

Syntax errors deal with things like punctuation or missing ( ) and typos. These are identified when you try to compile or run your program and must be corrected before the program will run.

Runtime errors do not cause an error at compile time, but occur when the program is executing. A common example is when a variable has a value of zero and the program tries to divide by it. The program may run successfully many times when the value is not zero, but will crash when it is zero.

Logic errors occur when the program produces unexpected results. These errors are typically harder to identify. You may think your program ran correctly because there were no identified errors.

You have to thoroughly understand what the program should do, produce, and display to effectively test an application and then find any errors. All program functionality must be adequately tested as well to ensure program correctness. This includes testing with valid and invalid data as well as "boundary" cases, which are those on the edge of program limitations.

> **Example:** If something should happen when a variable's value is less than 32, also check 31 and 33 as the boundary cases.

Testing should also ensure all features work in the way the user needs it to. Do not just test that all functions work. If a user needs to update a record, and uses three different features to accomplish this, be sure to test all three in the order the user would use them to ensure they work as needed, as well as testing them independently.

This is one reason the testing phase in the software development life cycle is so important. If you have a table of expected test results, and the program does not produce the expected value, you need to carefully check your code to find and correct the problem and be sure you understand what the program is supposed to do. The problem could be as simple as using "+" rather than "−" in a calculation, or you may use the wrong variable name in a program statement. The expected and actual test results can be used by a programmer to prove a program runs correctly.

The use of temporary print or DISPLAY statements inside a program helps with debugging. By printing out intermediate values to the screen or on paper or to indicate when a program reaches a certain section of code, the programmer can more easily identify the error. These extra print statements are removed after the error is resolved.

Programmers should add comment blocks to sections of code inside the program to indicate the functionality of those sections. Programmers should also complete the program documentation explaining the program features and how it should be used to meet the functionality originally identified in the problem definition. This could be in the form of a user guide to use in training those who will use the programs as well as "help" text.

# The Building Blocks of Programming

## Algorithms

One of the key facets of computational thinking is decomposition. This means breaking a problem down into smaller and smaller pieces. You keep breaking it down until you get to a point where you have a section small enough and defined well enough to code. Programs implement algorithms. The algorithm is the well-thought-out design to solve the customer's request. Software is written to run on computers to automate the processes for the problem the algorithm was designed to solve.

These algorithms have the potential to solve many problems once the programs are written for them to run. For example, a sorting algorithm is simple conceptually. Once it is programmed, an indefinite number of data sets can be sorted using it. As improvements are made to software and hardware, additional programming implementations are now feasible. For example, Chapter 7, Data and Information, includes information about "big data." These large data sets can now be processed using server farms and processing that distributes the data over multiple programs each executing a section of the data at the same time.

A section of code may work independently or can be used with other programming modules. These program modules read in values, make computations as needed, and produce output to automate processes. Programs may have a variety of data coming in (input) and going out (output). Input or output data could be in the form of text, video or images, audio files, or other formats, depending on the needs of the programming solution.

Basic computer architecture is based on the von Neumann design. Programs need input, the CPU (Central Processing Unit) to direct the execution of the commands, and memory and storage to produce output.

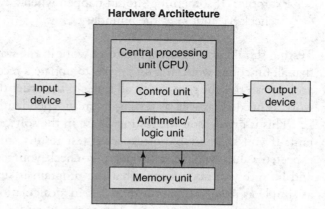

**Hardware Architecture**

## Variables

Variables are placeholders for values a program needs to use. A program may need variables for numbers, both integers and real numbers, as well as text fields. Programs can assign values to variables as well as update the value to be a new one. Variables can be used in expressions, both mathematical and textual. An important aspect of variables is naming them well. As discussed earlier, a descriptive name for a variable is "self-documenting" in that it describes the value or values that the variable holds.

## Procedures

Procedures are also called functions in some programming languages. These are sections of code that will be executed only when they are called by the main program or another procedure. They must be defined in a program before they can be called for the code to run in the program.

There are several benefits of using procedures.

- Reuse of code reduces the length and complexity of programs by not duplicating code.
- Procedures increase the ease of maintaining or fixing programs because you only have one place to update code rather than several.
- Use of shorter blocks of code that do only a few tasks makes it easier to understand the code.

When you find yourself needing the same section of code more than once in a program, that is a clue that you should put the code in a procedure. You can then use it as many times as needed in your program by calling it. Procedures should have descriptive names to help identify their purpose.

- **Calling**

  When the procedure is "called," the program will pause at that location, go and execute the code in the procedure, and then come back to the line of code after the call.

- **Parameters/Arguments**

   The use of parameters can make procedures more flexible. Parameters allow the calling program to send values to the procedure via arguments when the procedure is called. The values sent to the procedure can be different values each time, adding to the flexibility and ability for multiple calls.

   Note that the parameters sent to the procedure must be sent in the same order, if there are more than one, and be of the same data type (number or text field) that the procedure is expecting. The number and type of parameters are identified when the function is defined.

   Recall that abstraction is the removal of details to make something more general and therefore more flexible. This is exactly what procedures do in programs. Details are abstracted away so the procedure is more general and can be used multiple times.

   **Example:** DISPLAY ( ) is a built-in procedure. We do not need to know how this procedure is coded, only that we can use it multiple times and pass it different types and values to print, and that it works.

- **Return**

   Procedures may need to send data calculated or collected in the procedure back to the calling program. To do this, a "RETURN" statement is used in the procedure. When the return statement is run, processing the procedure is ended and control is returned to the calling program along with the value sent back.

# Data Types

The computer stores everything as 0s and 1s. Data types are the way computers assign some meaning to these binary digits. Doing this allows us to use those values in particular ways, such as numbers and text. There are three main data types you should understand for the exam: strings, integers, and fractional numbers.

## Strings

Strings are text fields and are denoted with quotation marks around the string field. Note that these could appear to be numbers, but if the field is defined as a string, then numbers will be considered to be text, like in a street address. In this case, you cannot use them in calculations because they are text fields, not numbers. There are many processes that are commonly done with strings, and most programming languages include pre-written procedures providing this functionality.

- Concatenating strings means "adding" them or "gluing" them together.
- Substrings are sections of strings.
- Common string operations in programs include determining if a certain character is in a string, where it is located, and adding or removing strings among many others.

## Integers

Integers are whole numbers. (They do not have a decimal point.) Integers can be used in mathematical operations and expressions, where strings (text fields) cannot. Different programming languages have maximum- and minimum-sized integers they can hold as a programming language limitation based on the size of the computer being used.

32-bit computers:

Minimum number = $-(2^{31})$

Maximum number = $2^{31} - 1$

64-bit computers:

Minimum number = $-(2^{63})$

Maximum number = $2^{63} - 1$

Once these limits are met, the program output is an "overflow" error. Generally, negative numbers are shown as positive and an expected positive number result is a negative number. You are not responsible for knowing what these maximum and minimum limits are, but you should understand the concept of a maximum and minimum number that computers can store and process and overflow.

**NOTE:** You do not need to know specific maximum and minimum integer ranges for the AP exam.

### "Fractional" Numbers

These are numbers with a decimal point and are often referred to as "floating point numbers." Even if a number has 0 (zero) for the decimal value, for example, 52.0, it is still considered to be a floating point number rather than an integer. These numbers can also be used in mathematical operations and expressions.

Floating point numbers are stored in memory in an imprecise way. For example, 1.0 could be stored as 0.99999994. This imprecision can cause a rounding issue, and could impact expected results from the program. This is why values representing money should not be stored using this data type. Be aware of how these are stored for the exam.

**NOTE:** Numbers that cannot be exactly represented by floating point numbers will *not* be on the AP exam.

# Foundations of Computer Programming

### Mathematical Processes

Most programming languages include math operations. For the AP exam, you need to understand the basic math functions of:

+    add

−    subtract

*    multiply

/    divide

MOD modulo math – returns just the remainder after dividing

### Assignment Statements

To assign a value to a variable, the variable is always on the left of the "←" sign. The programming language will evaluate the right-hand side of the equation and then place the value into the variable on the left-hand side of the assignment sign.

```
x ← 3.14 * 5
area ← PI * r * r
```

You will get an error if you write:

```
5 / 9 * (f - 32) → c
```

**NOTE:** The order of operations, PEMDAS, (see below), used in math is followed by programming languages. It is always better to use parentheses to ensure the correct order of processing for a mathematical expression.

| | |
|---|---|
| P | Parentheses |
| E | Exponents |
| M | Multiplication |
| D | Division |
| A | Addition |
| S | Subtraction |

f – 32 * 5 / 9 does not provide the same value as (f – 32) * (5 / 9)

## Boolean Values

Boolean values are one of the foundations of most computer code. Understanding Boolean is important for writing correct, readable, and efficient code. Remember Boolean values can only be true or false. Boolean expressions can only evaluate to either true or false. Relational operators are used with Boolean values. These are:

| | |
|---|---|
| = | equal |
| ≠ | not equal |
| > | greater than |
| < | less than |
| ≥ | greater than or equal to |
| ≤ | less than or equal to |

Two values are compared based on the relational operator and determined to be true or false. For example:

x ← 5
y ← 10
x > y evaluates to false because at this moment, x is 5 and y is 10. Five is not greater than 10.

## Compound Conditional Statements (AND, OR, NOT)

Boolean conditions can be simple or compound. Multiple conditions can be combined using the logical operators: AND, OR, and NOT.

To be true, both of the conditions on either side of the AND operator must be true when evaluated individually. In the example below, "licenseEligible" will be set to true if the age is greater than or equal to 16 and the Boolean variable "learnersPermit" is true. Otherwise, "licenseEligible" will be set to false.

```
licenseEligible ← (age ≥ 16) AND (learnersPermit)
```

For the OR condition, either or both of the conditions can be true for the condition to be true.

With the NOT operator, if a condition was true, then NOT makes it false. If a condition was false, then NOT makes it true.

# Lists

Lists are a collection of items, such as a grocery list or a playlist of music. A list in a program can be a collection of numbers, words, phrases, or a combination of these. Lists provide the ability to store more than one value in the same variable as long as the variable is defined as a list. This makes understanding lists when designing a solution and processing items in a list much easier. The list is a generalization (or abstraction) of a group of numbers and/or strings that can be used in certain ways.

### Index

Individual items in a list are accessed by their [index].

For the AP Computer Science Principles Exam, the list index starts at 1.

```
snacks[1] ← "popcorn"
snacks[2] ← "grapes"
```

If you attempt to reference a position in the list that does not exist, your program will end with an "index out of bounds" error.

```
snacks[9] does not exist.
```

### Length

The length of a list is the number of elements in the list. This number can be useful in processing items in a list. You can use references such as:

```
snacks[LENGTH(snacks)]
```

to access the last item in the list without having to know the length in advance.

### Checking Each Item in a List

```
FOR EACH item IN list
```

The above statement is a loop that will automatically iterate through each element in the list. The programmer chooses the name for the iteration variable "item". Each pass of the loop will assign the value at the next element to the variable "item".

Programmers can then add "IF" conditions or statements to process the elements. The FOR EACH loop stops after the last element in the list has been processed. You will not get an "index out of bounds" error when processing a list with the FOR EACH loop.

### Built-in Methods (Add, Append, Remove, Sort . . . )

Most programming languages will have built-in procedures, or "methods," to use with lists. These generally include functionality such as:

- Adding an item to a specific position in a list
- Appending an item to the end of the list
- Removing an item from a list
- Finding an item in a list
- Sorting a list

There are many others and you should become comfortable with looking these up for programming languages you use.

**NOTE:** The Exam Reference Sheet that you will be given for the exam has information about lists and the FOR EACH loop.

# APIs or "Libraries"

API stands for "Application Programming Interface." These are built-in programs written in a specific programming language to do commonly used functions, and are stored in a "library." The "DISPLAY" function is an example of a built-in API. You have to use it in the way specified, but you do not have to write the "behind the scenes" code to print in your program, greatly simplifying your program and the time it would take to write it.

Some of these built-in programs are already included in the programming language. There are others that you can "import" into your program when needed. You will need the exact name of the library to import, and you must import it before using any of the programs in the library in your program:

```
import math
num ← math.random(1,10)
```

The above code imports the "math" library into the program. It then generates a random number between 1 and 10 and stores it in the variable "num".

You can always look up the APIs/libraries for the programming language you are using in the program documentation. Documenting the procedures in an API and how to use them is important so others can use them successfully. Some APIs also connect various software components. For example, including Google Maps in an app can be accomplished using an API that allows the user of the app to use Google Maps without leaving the original app.

## ❯ Review Questions

### Concepts

1. What is a benefit of using a software development or engineering design process?

   (A) By following the process, the code will work the first time.
   (B) Using the process, the code will be efficient regardless of a programmer's experience.
   (C) The code will be developed in 50% less time using a development/design process.
   (D) The process is iterative, resulting in a better program.

2. Why is documentation important?

   (A) To explain a program's purpose and functionality
   (B) To make it easier to understand and modify the code later
   (C) To be useful for training people on how to use the program
   (D) All the above

3. What are variables used for in programs?

   (A) They hold values, numbers, or strings.
   (B) They link libraries of programs to the current program.
   (C) They indicate how long the fraction part of a real number is.
   (D) They hold the indices for a list.

4. Why should boundary values be tested?

   (A) Testing boundary values is not necessary.
   (B) To ensure they are identified as errors
   (C) To ensure warning messages are sent about the boundaries
   (D) To ensure the program does not include too few or too many elements

5. What is one way to debug a program?

   (A) Add temporary print messages to determine program values.
   (B) Test with different data values each time.
   (C) Document the error in the user guide and online help text.
   (D) Override the error with the correct value.

**6.** How can an individual element in a list be identified?

(A) Use the index or number of the element's position in the list.

(B) Use the built-in procedures for lists.

(C) Use the full list name.

(D) Use the list name plus the value in the list at the needed position.

**7.** How do parameters and arguments differ?

(A) The words can be used interchangeably.

(B) Parameters are sent to procedures where they are then used as arguments.

(C) Arguments are sent to procedures where they are then used as parameters.

(D) Arguments are the intermediate values in a calculation until the calculation is complete and then stored in the parameter.

**8.** What is a reason to use a procedure?

(A) When you need a section of code once in a program

(B) To avoid duplicating code

(C) To avoid a loop

(D) To use with a condition

**9.** How are assignment statements processed?

(A) The left side of the ← is processed and then assigned to the variable on the right.

(B) The right side of the ← is processed and then assigned to the variable on the left.

(C) Strings are processed first and then numbers.

(D) Numbers are processed first and then strings.

**10.** What is a benefit of understanding a problem before coding?

(A) A better designed program is created to handle all the needed functionality.

(B) Less testing is required.

(C) Little or no documentation is then needed.

(D) Users will not need training to use the program.

## Application of Concepts

**11.** Are the two conditional statements equivalent?

```
age > 42        NOT (age < 42)
```

(A) Yes

(B) No

(C) Only when age is a positive number

(D) Only when age is 0

**12.** What are the elements in the list "fruit" after the code below?

```
fruit ← ["grapes"]
APPEND (fruit, "bananas")
APPEND (fruit, "oranges")
APPEND (fruit, "apples")
REMOVE (fruit, 2)
INSERT (fruit, 3, "mango")
APPEND (fruit, "kiwi")
INSERT (fruit, 5, "blueberries")
REMOVE (fruit, 1)
```

(A) grapes, mango, apples, blueberries, kiwi

(B) oranges, mango, apples, blueberries, kiwi

(C) apples, mango, kiwi, blueberries

(D) bananas, mango, apples, kiwi, grapes

**13.** What is the result of executing the following code?

```
PROCEDURE LeapYear (year)
  IF a year MOD 400 = 0)
    DISPLAY (year, "is a leap year!")
  ELSE IF (year MOD 100 = 0)
    DISPLAY (year, "is not a leap year.")
  ELSE IF year MOD 4 = 0
    DISPLAY (year, "is a leap year!")
  ELSE
    DISPLAY ("Invalid year entered.")
DISPLAY ("Enter a year:")
yr ← INPUT( )
LeapYear(yr)
```

The user inputs the value 3004.

(A) 3004 is not a leap year.

(B) 204 is not a leap year.

(C) 3004 is a leap year!

(D) Invalid year entered.

**14.** Which block of code produces correct results?

```
Block 1:
IF (day = "Wed")
    setAlarm ← 8
ELSE IF (day = "Sat" OR day = "Sun")
    setAlarm ← 11
ELSE
    setAlarm ← 9


Block 2:
IF (day NOT("Sat") OR day NOT("Sun"))
    setAlarm ← 9
IF (day = "Wed")
    setAlarm ← 8
```

(A) Block 1
(B) Block 2
(C) Block 1 and Block 2
(D) Neither Block 1 nor Block 2

**15.** What is returned from the procedure below after the call weight (9, 10, 11)?

```
PROCEDURE weight(wt1, wt2, wt3)
{
IF (wt1 ≥ wt2 AND wt1 ≥ wt3)
    return wt1
ELSE IF (wt2 > wt3 OR wt2 > wt1)
    return wt2
ELSE
    return wt3
}
```

(A) 9
(B) 10
(C) 11
(D) 1011

# › Answers and Explanations

**1. D**—The steps in the software development and the engineering design processes are iterative, causing the developer to re-evaluate after testing to fix and improve the program. No process can ensure the code will be correct the first time, nor be efficient, nor decrease the development time by 50%, making D the correct answer.

**2. D**—Documentation is important to:
- Explain program's purpose and functionality.
- Make it easier to understand and modify the code later.
- Train people on how to use the program.

**3. A**—Variables are used to hold values, either numbers or strings, in programs.

**4. D**—Boundary values should be tested to ensure the program does not include too few or too many elements.

**5. A**—One way to debug a program is to add temporary print messages to determine program values.

**6. A**—An individual element in a list can be identified using the index or the number of the element's position in the list.

**7. C**—Arguments are sent to procedures where they are then used as parameters.

**8. B**—One reason to use a procedure is to avoid duplicating code.

**9. B**—Assignment statements process the right side of the ←, which is then assigned to the variable on the left.

**10. A**—One benefit of understanding a problem before coding is creating a better designed program to handle all the needed functionality.

**11. B**—The keyword NOT flips the value it references to its opposite. Therefore, if age is greater than 42, the opposite of that is age less than or equal to 42. Many students forget to include or remove the equals sign, =, when they apply the NOT operator. The two expressions do not match and the correct answer is B.

12. **B**—Our list starts with one element, "grapes". The APPEND operation adds the element to the end of the list. The INSERT operation places the element at the index position provided and moves elements to the right increasing the size of the list. The REMOVE operation deletes the element at the given index position and adjusts the remaining elements down a position. Lists for this course all begin with index position 1. Therefore, the correct answer is B.

13. **C**—The user keys in 3004 as the year to check. The procedure LeapYear(3004) is called with this value. The MOD function returns the remainder after dividing the two numbers. If the remainder is 0, then the year is a leap year. The ELSE IF statement that uses MOD 4 = 0 is true, so the year is a leap year and the correct message is printed. The correct answer is C.

14. **A**—Block 1 correctly sets the alarm time for every day of the week. Block 2 sets the correct alarm time for Monday to Friday. The weekend days do not have an alarm time set. The correct answer is A.

15. **B**—The first IF statement compares wt1 to the other two values. Since 9 is not greater than or equal to either value, the code moves on to compare wt2, which is 10. This condition is an OR so only one comparison needs to be true. While 10 is not greater than 11, it is greater than 9. Therefore the value of 10 for wt2 is returned. The correct answer is B.

# ❭ Rapid Review

Programs can be developed for almost any purpose, including for fun and for professional purposes. Advances in technology provide the ability to share programs or their output with users worldwide. They can become popular with widespread use very quickly. These advances have spread the development of new programs and technologies plus the expanded use of existing program applications to other businesses and organizations.

Software development should use an iterative development approach. It is a repeating process that continues until the users' requirements have been met. The process includes consulting with users, analyzing and designing a solution, coding the solution, and then testing. Modules of code can be developed and tested, and once they are working correctly, can then be incorporated into larger applications. Documenting the programs and providing external documentation for those using the system is very important to make it easier to maintain and modify the code as the users' needs change.

Software that is developed by teams with different skill sets and perspectives results in better designed and programmed solutions. Collaboration by the team has many benefits, including sharing the workload, creating better solutions than an individual probably would, and testing of each other's work.

Programs implement algorithms and use a variety of techniques, such as variables, procedures, and lists in their processing. Procedures are blocks of code that can be used repeatedly in programs. They can have parameters that provide a way for different values to be passed to them, and procedures can return values processed in the procedure back to the calling program. Using parameters makes a procedure more general, and therefore more abstract, by enabling it to be used with different values each time it is called to run. Lists, like a grocery list, can store many values in one variable name. Programming languages have built-in functions for common processing needs for lists, such as add, remove, insert, and search. The use of Application Program Interfaces (APIs) pulls in libraries of working code to an application saving time in the development process.

Just as algorithms can be written using sequential, selection, and iterative statements, programs use these same types of statements to implement the algorithms. Relational operators, such as ">" (greater than), produce Boolean results. These are always true or false. Compound conditions can be formed using "AND", "OR", and "NOT" with the relational operators.

Thorough testing of software is critical before releasing it for general use, although programs developed for personal use do not need the same level of testing and documentation. Debugging is the process of finding and fixing errors in the code.

# CHAPTER 10

# The Internet

**Big Idea # 6 of the AP Computer Science Principles Course**

**IN THIS CHAPTER**

**Summary:** The Internet is a network of networks. Anytime two devices are connected, a network has been created. Protocols determine how information is transferred across the Internet. During these transfers, cybersecurity protects our data using encryption.

**Key Ideas**
- ✪ The Internet has redundancy so it can still work if parts of it are not operational.
- ✪ It uses rules, or protocols, to send and receive data.
- ✪ Domain names are easy for people to remember and need to be translated to IP addresses.
- ✪ Cybersecurity protects our devices from unauthorized use.
- ✪ Cryptography uses encryption to protect sensitive information.
- ✪ Public key encryption is an open source algorithm in use today.

**Key Terms**

Asymmetric ciphers
Bandwidth
Brute Force attack
Certificate Authority (CA)
Ciphers

Cryptography
Cybersecurity
Decryption
Distributed Denial-
    of-Service attack
    (DDoS)

Domain names
Domain Name Service
  (DNS)
Encryption
End-to-end architecture
Fault tolerant
Frequency analysis
Host
Hypertext Markup
  Language (HTML)
Hypertext Transfer
  Protocol (HTTP)
Hypertext Transfer
  Protocol Secure
  (HTTPS)
Internet Engineering
  Task Force (IETF)
Internet Protocol (IP)
  address
IPv4/IPv6
Latency

Node
One-way function
Open Systems
  Interconnection (OSI)
  Modell
Packets
Phishing
Protocols
Public key encryption
Redundancy
Router
Secure Socket Layer/
  Transport Layer
  Security (SSL/TLS)
Symmetric ciphers
Transmission Control
  Protocol/Internet
  Protocol (TCP/IP)
Virus
World Wide Web (www)

# How the Internet Works

The Internet is a network of networks. The word *Internet* came from "*inter*connection of computer *net*works." Anytime two devices are connected, a network has been created. The Internet is very hardware-driven with wires, cables, and devices such as routers and servers. While some connections are wireless, there are still access points and cables that create the wireless network. The level of collaboration we have today is largely due to the Internet. People from across the globe can work together, create together, and edit together because of these connections.

### End-to-End Architecture

The processing of Internet traffic is done at the sending and receiving locations. At the sending location, the information, such as a web page, is broken into smaller packets of the same size (except possibly the last one, which could be smaller). The packets are sent on their way to the destination location along different routes. The intermediate routers along the path move the packets to the next destination on the path. The packets are put back together at the destination. This is called an end-to-end architecture, because the processing is done at each end, nothing happens in the middle except moving it along to the next location.

### Fault Tolerant

There is a lot of redundancy or duplication built into the Internet. This means that if one point goes down and is not working, then the traffic will be redirected to a different node to get to its ultimate destination. It is often referred to as "fault tolerant" due to these multiple connections and paths. This duplication also enables the Internet to scale up by increasing the routers and paths to be able to manage more devices and more traffic.

## Packet Switching

Information is separated into fixed length packets. The packets are sent to their destination via multiple routes. Their header information includes the destination address and where to place the information in the packet in the final reconstruction. Once all packets have arrived at the destination, they are reassembled in order.

## Nodes and Hosts

Every device on a network is called a "node" or "host". When a device connects to the Internet, it is given an "address" similar to the idea of a mailing address given homes and businesses. These nodes or devices can be anywhere in the world. The addresses enable devices to find and communicate with each other. The address is called an Internet Protocol (IP) address. It's how the Internet knows where to route information.

## Protocols

Protocols are a set of rules. These are needed so different equipment made by different companies can communicate with each other. Whether a connection is wired or wireless, before the packets of information can travel across networks, a common protocol, or a set of rules for transmitting and receiving these packets of data must be used.

The protocols are created by a committee of representatives from different industries who agree on the set of rules for everyone to follow. This committee is the Internet Engineering Task Force (IETF), which is part of the Internet Society. The Internet does not belong to any one country or individual, but its use needs to be agreed on and managed. These standards are continually reviewed and modified as needed to enable new uses for the Internet, and to take advantage of new hardware and other tools to facilitate its structure.

Initially, various businesses were creating their own protocols to use on the Internet. This resulted in incompatibility and people were unable to send or receive data across the different protocols. The standards are now open and available to all to ensure people can communicate across the Internet. This agreement to use an open standard enabled the growth of the Internet.

As an example of this growth, so many devices that need IP addresses exist globally that the current protocol, IPv4 (version 4) is being replaced by IPv6 (version 6). IPv6 uses 128 bits, organized into 8 groups of 16, written in hexadecimal. It provides $3.4 \times 10^{38}$ possible IP addresses versus the 4.3 billion addresses that IPv4 provided.

**NOTE:** You do *not* need to know specific details of the standards for addresses on the exam.

One of the oldest protocols is TCP/IP. TCP creates the packets and reassembles them. IP moves the packets through the network to their target location. It stands for:

**T**ransmission
**C**ontrol
**P**rotocol
/
**I**nternet
**P**rotocol

## Open Systems Interconnection (OSI) Model

OSI is not an operational protocol but is a model. It provides the layers needed for different systems to communicate for those creating different protocols. There are seven layers and each layer deals with an aspect of network communications. A layer is served by the layer below it and serves the layer above it. Also be aware that only layers one, two, and three (from the bottom) are mandatory for data transmissions. The other layers may not all be used in simpler applications. Note how TCP/IP aligns with the OSI model with the top three layers combined into one.

| OSI Model | | TCP/IP |
|---|---|---|
| Application | | Application |
| Presentation | | |
| Session | | |
| Transport | | Transport |
| Network | | Internetwork |
| Data link | | Link and physical |
| Physical | | |

**NOTE:** The details of how each layer of the OSI model works is *not* on the AP exam.

Another frequently used protocol developed by the IETF is Simple Mail Transfer Protocol (SMTP). SMTP is one of the available electronic mail protocols.

## Hypertext Transfer Protocol (HTTP) and Hypertext Transfer Protocol Secure (HTTPS)

HTTP controls how web page data is requested, sent, and received from the browsers and servers where the web pages are stored.

HTTPS should be used for any secure transaction. These include financial data, medical data, and sites that require a password.

## Bandwidth

Bandwidth is the data transfer rate, meaning the amount of data that can be moved across the network in a set amount of time. The data is measured in bits, and you often see it noted as "bps" (bits per second) or now more commonly Mb/s (megabits per second). Schools, businesses, and individuals purchase "bandwidth" usually via a set fee per month from an Internet Service Provider (ISP). You may hear it referred to as a 100-meg pipe or 150-meg pipe.

There are many free websites that will measure your upload and download speeds as well as show your Internet usage over time. Usually the download speed is faster than the upload speed because people usually download content to their devices more often than upload. This is how you can determine when to plan to upgrade your bandwidth by purchasing a faster transfer rate.

## Latency

Latency is the time delay between the request for data and the receipt of it. It's the time you wait after you hit "Enter" and when the new information requested is displayed on your screen.

## Domain Names

Domain names are the website names that use words and letters to describe them. It's easy for people to remember names, such as google.com and collegeboard.org. However, the Internet needs them to be in number format for the IP address, as discussed previously.

### Syntax/Format

Domain names have a defined hierarchical format, which makes it easy to organize and add new names:

- The last level on the far right, for example ".com", is the top-level domain (TLD). http://anysite.anywhere.com
- Each successive level to the left goes up one level. Thus, the next level to the left (delineated by periods) is the second-level domain, e.g., .anywhere.
- The one to the left of that is the third-level domain, .anysite in our example, and so on.

Multiple levels are not always present for every domain name: http://anysite.com

Any information to the right of the top-level domain provides the path for folders and the ultimate filename. This information is not always present in a uniform resource locator (URL): http://anysite.com/where/location.docx

### Domain Name Service

The Domain Name Service (DNS) translates the site name in text format to a numeric IP address. There are servers that maintain lists with the hostname and its corresponding IP address. For example, google.com is translated to: 2001:4860:4860::8888 in IPv6 format. The DNS servers are located in multiple locations around the world. Everyone is mapped to the one closest to them, but if one goes down or does not maintain that particular web address, requests are sent be sent to another DNS server.

The DNS system provides multiple benefits including allowing sites to grow or change locations while the domain name remains the same. The website can move to a different host server without impacting the ability to find the web server that hosts the information requested.

## World Wide Web

The World Wide Web (WWW) is an application that runs on the Internet. Many people use the terms "WWW" and "Internet" interchangeably, but they are two different things. The World Wide Web is a collection of web pages, or documents, written in hypertext markup language (HTML). Our browsers read the HMTL code to know how to display the web page.

There are standards for how the web browsers and servers on the Web work:

- **Hypertext Transfer Protocol (HTTP)**
  - HTTP controls how web page data is requested, sent, and received.
- **Secure Sockets Layer/Transport Layer Security (SSL/TLS)**
  - These provide a secure connection to send sensitive data between two sites. The SSL has fallen out of use due to a new vulnerability and Transport Layer Security (TLS) has replaced it.

**NOTE:** You will *not* be asked how SSL/TLS works on the AP exam.

# Security on the Internet

### Cybersecurity

Cybersecurity protects our electronic devices and networks from attacks and unauthorized use. These attacks can come in many forms and can have a major impact on those affected. Many of them come into a network or device through email. An unsuspecting person clicks on a link that downloads a computer virus or other form of malware (the term "malware" comes from "malicious software"). Different types of attacks cause different problems. Data may be damaged or the device may be used to further spread the malware.

A Distributed Denial-of-Service attack (DDoS) occurs when the targeted web server is flooded with so many requests that it cannot handle them all. Responses from the web server become very slow and the server can ultimately crash, meaning it stops responding to all requests.

Phishing attacks create email and/or websites that look exactly like a legitimate site hoping to induce a person to click on it. These sites often prompt a user for their password, credit card number, or other sensitive data while appearing to be a valid transaction. The password or other personal information is then used and/or sold for illegal use.

Computer viruses are like human viruses. They attach themselves to. or are part of, an infected file. There are many types that can damage, delete, or steal your files and use your system to spread to other devices. Do not click on files in an email from people you do not know or even from someone you know, if you are not expecting an attachment.

Computer worms are similar to viruses in the damage they can cause, but they are not part of an infected file. These are separate files that can make endless copies of themselves and do not need a file to be opened to spread.

The solution for computer malware is to use antivirus software, firewalls, and caution when downloading or opening files from an unknown or unexpected source. Keep current with installing updates for your antivirus software and your operating system.

## Cryptography

Cryptography is the writing of secret codes. It has been used for thousands of years and is the reason we are able to have secured online shopping and keep our data in "cloud" accounts secured with our passwords today. Converting a message, also called "plaintext", is called encryption. Deciphering the encrypted message is called decryption.

Ciphers are coded messages and all ciphers have two parts:

- **Key:** Allows the creation of secret messages
- **Algorithm:** The set of steps used to transpose the message to be unreadable to anyone but the person who holds the key

Julius Caesar credited with the Caesar Cipher, one of the first ciphers, which is a secret code system. It shifted letters over three spaces and took 800 years to be broken. It is a "symmetric cipher," which means that the same key is used to encrypt and decrypt the message. Asymmetric ciphers use different keys to encrypt and decrypt a message.

**NOTE:** Specific encryption techniques are *not* on the AP exam.

### Attacks on Internet Security

#### Brute Force Attack

Brute force searches involve testing every possible key to break the code. This type of attack can be time-consuming. With today's security, we do not have the processing power to break long codes in a reasonable amount of time.

#### Frequency Analysis

Another way codes were broken involved frequency analysis. This involved knowing which letters in a given language appeared more often. In English, the letter "e" is used most often and the letter "t" is the next most common letter. Knowing this, ciphers were decoded by identifying which letters appeared most often in the coded message. These were then substituted for the most common letters in the language used to aid in breaking the code.

After this, code makers used multiple alphabets to flatten out the letter frequencies. These are called polyalphabetic substitution ciphers. A different alphabet is used to encrypt each letter. A keyword determines which alphabet is used. These were eventually broken because patterns were identified and then brute force or frequency analysis techniques could be used to break the code.

Stenography is the coding of messages into images. It is often referred to as "hiding in plain sight."

## Public Key Encryption

Today's algorithms use open standards, meaning the algorithms used are open to everyone and are discussed by experts and interested parties and known by all. The key is what keeps our information secret until the person it is intended for decrypts it. In this case, the public key is published to anyone. Messages are decrypted using a private key. This is considered a one-way function. That means the function is easy in one direction and difficult in the other. This algorithm becomes intractable because it creates such large numbers that a brute force attack cannot break the code. Remember that intractable problems mean a solution exists, but our current-day computers do not have adequate memory or time to solve it.

**NOTE:** The cryptography algorithms are based on mathematical functions, and these are *not* covered on the AP exam.

## Securing the Internet

The Internet is based on a "trust" model. This means that digital certificates can be purchased from Certificate Authorities (CAs), which identify trusted sites. They issue certificates that businesses, organizations, and individuals load to their websites. The certificates verify to Web browsers that the encryption keys belong to the business thereby enabling e-commerce and the sending and receiving of secure documents.

**NOTE:** The details of how CAs work is *not* on the AP exam.

# › Review Questions

## Concepts

1. What is a computer network?

   (A) A way to connect devices to share data
   (B) Web pages that can be shared globally
   (C) A dedicated line from one computer to another
   (D) A set of passwords needed to access other computers

2. What is the name for a setup where processing is done at the sending and receiving locations?

   (A) LAN
   (B) Point-to-point environment
   (C) End-to-end architecture
   (D) Redundant organization

3. What is the number assigned to devices on the Internet?

   (A) Internet Protocol address
   (B) Domain name
   (C) Host name
   (D) Router instructions

4. What does a DNS server do?

   (A) Determines if a website is secure
   (B) Transmits information securely
   (C) Translates an IP address to a website name
   (D) Translates a website name to the IP address

5. Why is the Internet considered to be fault tolerant?

   (A) It has dedicated lines between devices.
   (B) It has duplicate paths to all locations.
   (C) It is secured against all threats.
   (D) It is open to anyone with a connection.

6. What is the World Wide Web?

   (A) A collection of wires and cables to connect devices
   (B) Another name for the Internet
   (C) A way to search for and share documents and resources
   (D) A browser

7. Which of the following is an example of a Distributed Denial of Service (DDoS) attack?

   (A) Domain name server (DNS) attack
   (B) Cybersecurity attack
   (C) Brute force attack
   (D) Cryptography attack

8. What is a symmetric key used for?

   (A) Sending and receiving information from the Web
   (B) Encrypting data
   (C) Decrypting data
   (D) Encrypting and decrypting data

9. Cryptography today uses which of the following?

   (A) Published algorithms available to all
   (B) Algorithms known by only a few members of the IETF
   (C) The Caesar Cipher
   (D) Undecidable algorithms

## Application of Concepts

10. Which of the following is true about packets?

    (A) Packets leave and arrive at their destination at the same time.
    (B) Packets travel along different paths to their destination.
    (C) Each router decrypts the packets to confirm their destination.
    (D) If a packet does not arrive at the destination, the entire message is resent.

11. Which of the following is false about Domain Name System (DNS) servers?

    (A) There is only one DNS server; if it goes down, Internet traffic stops.
    (B) IP addresses are linked to domain names by the DNS.
    (C) They use IPv4 and IPv6 formats.
    (D) DDoS attacks sometimes take advantage of DNS to flood the target site.

12. Why does the IPv6 format use letters and numbers?
    (A) The IP address is numerical and is linked to the domain name, which is text-based.
    (B) It is like a street address with a number and name combination for each location.
    (C) It is based on hexadecimal, which uses numbers 0–9 and letters A–F.
    (D) When the IP address has to be manually entered, it can be keyed in more easily.

13. Which of the following is false about HTTPS?
    (A) HTTPS uses Certificate Authorities (CAs) to verify a site's identity.
    (B) HTTPS encrypts data before it is separated into packets.
    (C) HTTPS ensures the secure sharing of data.
    (D) HTTPS trades faster performance for more security.

## › Answers and Explanations

1. **A**—Computer networks connect devices.

2. **C**—An end-to-end architecture is where processing is done at the sending and receiving locations.

3. **A**—The Internet Protocol (IP) address is the number assigned to devices on the Internet.

4. **D**—The DNS server translates a website name to an IP address.

5. **B**—The Internet is considered to be fault tolerant because if one path is down, it has another route it can take.

6. **C**—The World Wide Web is a way to search for and share documents.

7. **B**—A Distributed Denial of Service (DDoS) attack is an example of a cybersecurity attack.

8. **D**—A symmetric key is used for both encrypting and decrypting data.

9. **A**—Cryptography today uses published algorithms available to all.

10. **B**—Packets travel along different paths to their final destination. They do not arrive at the same time, nor does the router decrypt messages. Only the packets that are missing are resent, not the entire stream.

11. **A**—There are multiple DNS servers located in different places around the world.

12. **C**—The new IPv6 format is a 128-bit number that uses eight groups of four hexadecimal digits. Hexadecimal uses 0–9 and A–F to represent 16 digits.

13. **D**—HTTPS provides a secure environment but does not slow down the performance of Internet-based exchanges.

## 〉 Rapid Review

The Internet is a network of networks, which enables people across the globe to be connected. Its structure provides multiple paths to many hosts, so if one path is down, information can travel back and forth over a different route. These main hosts can be regional or local Internet Service Providers (ISPs) that provide Internet connections to homes and businesses. This redundancy makes the Internet "fault tolerant," which makes it more reliable. This structure also enables the Internet to scale up as more devices join and more routes and connection points are needed.

There are rules, called protocols, for connecting and communicating on the Internet, so the correct sites can be found. Each time a device connects to the Internet, it is assigned an Internet Protocol (IP) address. So many devices were connecting, that a new protocol design, IPv6, was established to have more numbers available to assign to devices. The DNS (Domain Name System) translates an easy to remember domain name, such as a website name, to an IP address, which is a set of numbers. The Internet is organized in a very hierarchical way through the domain name system and IP addresses.

The Internet uses an "end-to-end architecture" meaning at the sending and receiving ends information is broken into packets, sent along different routes to its destination, and then reconfigured at the destination, Transmission Control Protocol before (TCP). IP is the standard used for transmitting information along the paths. So together, TCP/IP represents the standards used for sending information to the correct locations across all the Internet pathways. Latency is the delay that occurs from the time a request for information is sent until it is received. Bandwidth is the amount of data that can be sent or received in a set period of time.

Cybersecurity has become a critical field since the Internet was not designed to be a secure system. While antivirus software and firewalls can prevent many types of malware, hackers often trick people into clicking on unsafe sites or documents using phishing techniques to spread viruses and worms. Distributed denial-of-service (DDoS) attacks flood a targeted system with requests until it cannot handle them and ultimately crashes or slows to a crawl.

Cryptography is a new field that deals with ensuring data is secured via encryption methods before being transmitted across the Internet. Older methods used symmetric encryption where the same key was used to encrypt and decrypt the data. Securely sharing the key used for encrypting and decrypting was an issue with this method.

The current technique is public key encryption, which uses an asymmetric system meaning one key is used to encrypt data and another is used to decrypt it. The key is divided into a public and a private part. The public keys are openly published and available to anyone. The algorithm uses the public key to encrypt, and the receiver decrypts with their private part of the key. This makes it an intractable process to decrypt. Recall from Big Idea #4: Algorithms, that intractable means it takes too much memory or time to process. As advances in computer processing power are made, this method may become possible to break, but for now, our data and financial transactions on the Internet are secure.

The Internet is based on a "trust" model meaning Certificates of Authority (CAs) are issued that ensure the public keys shared by sites we want to do secure processing with are legitimate. If we are buying a product online, our web browsers can trust that the company site is the correct one based on their CA, and we can proceed with our credit card transaction.

# CHAPTER 11

# Global Impact

Big Idea # 7 of the AP Computer Science Principles Course

**IN THIS CHAPTER**

**Summary:** Computing has impacted all aspects of our lives, from communication to shopping to research. It has provided ways to share and innovate. With this technology comes privacy, security, legal, and ethical concerns.

**Key Ideas**
✪ New technologies allow new ways to communicate and interact.
✪ Sharing data allows citizen scientists to participate in identification and problem solving.
✪ There are positive and negative effects of many computing innovations.
✪ Licensing of people's work and providing attribution are essential.

**Key Terms**

Asynchronous
Creative Commons Licensing
Crowdfunding
Crowdsourcing
Data mining

Digital Millennium
   Copyright Act (DMCA)
Machine learning
Open source
Plagiarism
Synchronous

**NOTE:** Some aspects of Big Idea #7: Global Impact are assessed in your written response for the Explore Performance Task. Therefore, only 10% of the multiple-choice questions on the AP exam address Global Impact.

# New Ways to Communicate and Interact

Because of the Internet and the World Wide Web (www), people can share, question, post, collaborate, and create with individuals around the world. Many new ways to communicate have been developed. These include email, Short Message Service (SMS, which is texting), the ability to send photos and videos, and online chat used as a "help" service to potential customers or users of a website. Texting and chat both initially had message size limits leading to the development of shorthand such as "ty" for "thank you" to save characters. Emoticons also became commonplace to help ensure people understood the emotion around a message.

The Internet provides the opportunity to communicate with people across the globe. People can connect and communicate every day, at all hours of the day. Messages can be sent at the convenience of the sender, and the receiver can check them and reply as time permits. Time differences do not matter. This is referred to as **asynchronous** communication. Communications (data) are sent occasionally rather than as a constant stream.

## Video Conferencing and Video Chat

Video conferencing and video chat are examples of **synchronous** communication because all parties are seeing the same thing at the same time. While there could be a small delay, it is still a synchronous transmission. Video conferencing has had a major impact on businesses because employees do not have to travel as much to visit customers and vendors, using video conferencing instead. Employees are also able to work remotely and can still participate in meetings via video conference. (They should remember to change out of their pajamas before the meeting if they are working from home!) Consultations with medical experts located anywhere can be conducted via video conferencing as well.

## Social Media

Social media sites, such as Twitter, Facebook, SnapChat, and Instagram, as well as blogs have changed the way many people share information. News of events can be shared in "real time," meaning as events are happening, by people who are attending the event. Videos and stories go "viral," meaning they quickly get many views and are shared for even more views. These features allow us to have a better understanding of other parts of the world as well as be entertained. However, remember that certain governments block some or all content from the Internet for their citizens.

**NOTE:** Questions about specific social media sites will *not* be on the AP exam.

One unintended result of the rise of social media is **cyberbullying.** Some people use social media to bully others by posting anonymously, spreading false information, and having others pick up and continue to share the falsehood. This is a serious negative impact of the use of the Internet and social media.

## Cloud Computing

Cloud computing offers new ways for people to communicate, making collaboration easier and more efficient. Storing documents in the "cloud" simply means they are stored on a computer server at a location different than where the owner of the files is located. The documents are accessible via an Internet connection to anyone with verified access to it. This provides several benefits, including the ability for multiple people to update one document at the same time. This eliminates the problem of keeping track of multiple versions of the document—a major headache in the past. People could accidentally overwrite other's people's changes or be viewing an out-of-date version.

Another benefit of cloud computing is that people can access the document stored in the cloud from any device, at any time, at any location that has Internet access. This also allows multiple experts to easily evaluate and review documents, leading to better outcomes, whether it's evaluating a medical condition, a business plan, or a group project for a class.

## Changes in the Way Businesses Operate

The World Wide Web (www), an application running under the Internet, makes it easy to share documents, videos, and all types of computing artifacts as well as create interactive sites where others can provide opinions, advice, and suggestions. This has changed the way businesses and organizations operate. Cloud computing is one example. Businesses have also been able to allow employees to work remotely and conduct meetings via technology tools such as video conferencing or other tools such as Google Hangouts, Facetime, and Skype. They can also use features such as YouTube live to telecast information. This saves money on travel expenses and can provide flexibility for employees.

The Internet also provides many distractions that can, in turn, hurt productivity. Studies have shown the impact on businesses with loss of productivity by employees watching major sporting events that occur during the workday, such as World Series games.

## Health Care

Medical files, test results, and x-rays can be digitized and sent to specialists in any part of the world for evaluation. Physicians are able to collaborate with experts located anywhere in the world and can be looking at the same test results at the same time.

## Online Learning

Online learning is an education model that would not be possible without the tools of communication available via the Internet. Now, you can have classmates from anywhere in the world. You can also attend class if you are in a different location other than your teacher. Teachers are able to do a combined lesson with a class elsewhere in the world using tools such as Google Hangouts, Facetime, or Skype. This can expose students to a global perspective that can impact people's understanding of each other, their cultures, and the challenges they face plus things they have in common.

# Access to Information

Through the Internet and the World Wide Web, we have vast amounts of data at our fingertips. This allows us to find out just about any fact in a few seconds no matter where we are. We can not only easily find out how to get from point A to point B, but we also can find out about traffic congestion along the way—real-time data that could not have been collected before the Internet.

The sharing of huge amounts of public data by organizations, such as the U.S. government, provides the opportunity for anyone to search for information or help solve problems. In addition, the availability of open databases in a variety of fields—including science, entertainment, sports, and business, has benefited people everywhere. People identify issues and opportunities leading to new facets and products for research, production, and sales.

## Global Positioning Systems

Global positioning systems (GPS) uses satellites to create maps of roads and terrain. There are also GPS systems specifically designed to navigate bodies of water. These maps are displayed on GPS devices and smart devices. Rather than having to look up routes on maps prior to departure, GPS has changed how we travel to unfamiliar destinations. We can listen to the step-by-step directions, know what lane to be in for an upcoming turn, find out about delays before we reach them, and request a different route as well as find places of interest including tourist destinations along with restaurants, gas stations, or other necessities along a travel route. The military has more precise maps, but the ones available to consumers are still precise within 3 to 4 meters. There are driving, walking, and bus paths enabling travelers everywhere to get to their destinations even without speaking the local language or being able to read maps or signs, or ask for directions.

## Access to Practical Information for Our Lives

Many aspects of our lives are much easier today because of the easy access to data that the Internet provides. This can range from shopping, entertainment, and sports sites to price comparisons. We can research health symptoms and medical treatment and find vetted sources for research. We can also find online classes taught by instructors anywhere in the world, as well as illegal sites and transactions as we pick up viruses and other malware along the way.

So many devices can now connect to the Internet and perform small tasks that a new category has been created and is referred to as the "Internet of Things," or IoT. Many of these involve apps that are downloaded to smart devices such as phones and tablets. They connect to your home thermostat, coffeemaker, refrigerator, and car, among other things, to track and allow the user to modify their settings.

Many of these also are categorized as assistive technologies to help people with some disabilities to better navigate the world and keep up with their appointments and medications. Assistive technologies can even report results, such as pacemaker and insulin pump readings to doctors remotely.

## Finding and Evaluating Online Data

In fact there is so much data available online that the problem is knowing how to find what you need. Search engines typically tell us how many millions of results met our search criteria. Their algorithms then determine which ones to return to us in what order. We have to learn to effectively use advanced search tools, keywords, and filtering techniques to narrow down these results to a manageable number containing the information we need. There are online databases of vetted materials that help all researchers as well.

We then have to determine if the information we are viewing was created by a credible source. Learning to evaluate the sources or only using vetted material is a necessary skill. Being able to find and evaluate the credentials of an article or site determine the effectiveness of the material being reviewed.

The Internet and the World Wide Web make it very easy to find information and thereby copy and paste it into another document. Be aware that it is equally easy to test for plagiarism. Always cite your sources for work and ideas that are not your own.

### Search Trends and Analytics

Social media sites as well as search engines publish what the most frequent searches and posts are about. They are able to identify when more people than usual are watching a video or searching for a topic. The companies use this information to predict trends and then use their information about related topics to share with those searching and researching. Similarly, analytics identify trends for marketing purposes and help businesses determine what and where customers are searching for their products and their competitors' products, how long an item sits in a virtual shopping cart, and when people buy.

### Data Mining and Machine Learning

Data mining is a field of study that analyzes large data sets. Companies may use the results to determine when to offer a discount for specific products. Machine learning is a subset of data mining. Machine learning uses algorithms to analyze data and predict behavior. Companies then use it to target ads or products to you based on your prior searches or purchasing behavior. It can also be used for a potential fraud alert if your bank notes unusual activity on your account. The machine has "learned" your usual patterns and issues an alert if something is different. If the software used is able to predict more accurately over time, then it is considered machine learning.

Science and business have both benefited from these new sources of information. Machine learning has been able to predict when someone will need a new battery for a pacemaker or drop out of a research study so those leading the project can work more closely with the person to try and prevent it. The medical field is working to identify risk factors for diseases to help those at risk to make changes to reduce their chance of contracting the disease. For the business world, retaining employees is important to keep knowledge and the company's investment in training the employee in-house. The use of computers to evaluate job candidates has resulted in a higher retention rate.

### Open Source Software

Not only do we have access to data, but to software as well. "Open source" software is software that is freely shared, updated, and supported by anyone who wants to do so. The availability of this software for everyone has greatly expanded people's abilities to participate in a variety of tasks that many would not have been able to participate in otherwise. Allowing many to develop the software ensures a better product with the ideas and solutions to problems from many perspectives. It also is generally a less error-prone product because of all the people testing the software.

Of course, there are also concerns if someone takes code from these openly available programs and either uses it with additional code they wrote, markets it in some way claiming it as their own, or inserts malware into the open source code thereby impacting everyone who then downloads it.

# Access to a Wider Audience

The Internet has created a way for easy access to worldwide audiences. Providers of goods and services can directly access their customers, eliminating the importance of all types of "middlemen" from brick-and-mortar stores to publishers and music distributors to radio-dispatched taxis. This has changed the way we shop, get our entertainment, schedule a ride, and even obtain financing for projects. But this also raises security, privacy, and ethical concerns related to many aspects and uses of the Internet. Cybersecurity has a global impact because now anyone from anywhere can attempt to gain unauthorized entry to someone else's computer, data, servers, or network.

### E-Commerce

A huge impact of the World Wide Web is the ability to sell products to a worldwide consumer base. E-Commerce is a business model that became possible because of the Internet and the Web. We can shop via companies that are exclusively online and many local and national stores now have online stores in addition to their "brick-and-mortar" locations.

### Entertainment

Entertainment has also been impacted by the global reach of the Internet. Many stars and celebrities of today got their start by posting videos of their performances. They garnered enough attention to catch the eye of the entertainment industry, thus launching their career even further. This works for musicians, comedians, and artists as well as actors. Entertainment is a huge business with movies, books, and music, available for streaming, downloading, or watching on the web at any time of the day or night. This can be both a good or bad thing, depending on how people manage their screen time.

# Crowdsourcing

Crowdsourcing allows people to share information and ask the "crowd"—anyone who accesses the site—for feedback, help problem-solving, employment, or funding. Another use of crowdsourcing is when scientists share data and ask nonscientists, or "citizen scientists", to look for and report on patterns or other interesting features of the data or to "donate" computer time during periods of time their machine is inactive. This helps to "scale up" processing capability at little to no cost to the organization seeking the resources.

Examples of "citizen" science include monitoring monarch butterfly migrations, recording plastics that wash up on beaches worldwide, and classifying galaxies! These efforts can help focus further research on these features or newly generated and identified information. People are also willing to help with documentation, with identifying photos, and with all types of assistance as additional examples of crowdsourcing. These collaborative efforts help people and society as a whole with discoveries and advances in many fields. As people move toward "always-on" mobile devices, new applications are being created to take advantage and utilize this capability. For example, there are apps that measure the number of steps the "device" (actually the person carrying the device) takes a day.

Crowdfunding helps inventors, individuals, and businesses fund their ventures with a little bit of money from many sources. The Internet has made it possible now to easily see from anywhere in the world what new innovations or events people are trying to raise money for and to bring to market.

# Legal and Ethical Concerns

### Creative Commons

Creative Commons provides a way for creators of software, images, music, and videos to share their creations with stipulations for sharing and permission from the author clearly indicated. Creative Commons provides six levels of licensing that the owner/creator decides for their work. These levels include use with and without attribution, the ability to modify with and without attribution, and whether someone other than the original author can sell it.

Digital data is easy to find, copy, and paste, so ensuring you have written permission from the creator or owner is important. Just as it is easy to find many computer artifacts on the Web., it is also very easy for people to search for their artifacts to see if someone is using them without permission. If you use something without permission, be prepared for official consequences, including a fine and orders to remove it among other actions.

## Digital Millennium Copyright Act

The Digital Millennium Copyright Act (DMCA) was signed in 1998. Its purpose was to strengthen legal protection for intellectual property, particularly with the use of the Internet. Lack of knowledge about the copyright laws does not excuse the offender from legal ramifications. Digital items you purchase, such as music and software, have licensing information on their packaging. Be sure to read it before making additional copies to share.

There have been many examples of illegal downloads and sharing of music, games, and videos, particularly with the now defunct application, Napster. This and other peer-to-peer networks are used to illegally share files of all types. This is a serious legal issue. While doing a Google search recently, the message below was at the bottom of the results page:

> In response to a complaint we received under the US Digital Millennium Copyright Act, we have removed 1 result(s) from this page. If you wish, you may read the DMCA complaint that caused the removal(s) at LumenDatabase.org.

## Other Legal and Ethical Concerns

"Mashups" where people combine content created by others is a copyright concern, especially if they earn money from doing so. There have been lawsuits challenging when someone's intellectual property is changed enough that someone does not have to compensate them for using it.

Even when people have approved access to information, choosing to use that access in legal and ethical ways matters. Often, digital innovations become accepted with widespread use before legal implications can be determined. There always seems to be something in the news where someone shared, used, or sold information for unethical purposes. These instances cause the legal system to then create laws regarding such use. Often, damage is already done before that can happen. On the other side of the coin, censorship of digital information by government, businesses, or individuals is also harmful and raises ethical, if not legal, concerns.

## Use of Personal Data

There are times when our personal data is used, either with or without our permission. Sometimes, the information will be rolled into big data sets for use at an aggregate level, and other times, it is used at a more personal level, such as businesses sending special offers to people who visit their stores a certain number of times. Both of these raise privacy and potential security concerns if identifying information about us is still available in the aggregate or local data sets. While the perks of being a frequent customer can be nice, if your information is compromised or used against you, such as robbing your house because you posted you were out to dinner, the benefit is not worth it.

Targeted advertising can be useful when you are searching for something, like that perfect gift. However, the downside is that you may only be shown items the algorithm thinks you would like and you may never see other items. This limits your access to other products and information and impacts those potential businesses.

There are ways to search in anonymous mode to prevent this tracking. Many web browsers now have "incognito" or "private" modes so web searches and file downloads are not recorded on the web history. There are also ways to be more anonymous to avoid tracking by websites, such as blocking cookies, installing add-ons to prevent them from tracking your device, and using proxy servers among other techniques. These are constantly evolving as other software is developed to get around them.

It is a constant challenge, because sometimes by accident, and sometimes on purpose, all the data that has been collected about us is released to those who should not have it or to the world at large. When this involves medical information; financial information, such as credit card numbers; and personal information including Social Security numbers—it puts our safety, personal and digital, at risk.

## Access to the Internet

Technology has had a major impact on the world, enabling innovation through the sharing of resources and artifacts. It also allows us to virtually meet with people from anywhere. It is helping us on the path of becoming a true global society.

But, while the Internet and the World Wide Web have had a global impact on the ease of sharing and collaborating, it is important to remember that not all areas of the world have the same access. Rural and remote areas often have limited, as in slower or even no, access to the Internet. Other areas are poor and do not have the infrastructure to support digital access. There are those who cannot afford the fees to connect to the Internet and the Web or buy the devices to do so. All of these create a "digital divide" between those with resources and those without.

The elimination of "net neutrality" has the potential to create an additional digital divide where those with the funding have faster and better access to the Internet and the Web. While the Internet and the World Wide Web are not "owned" by anyone, each government determines the access its citizens may have and many businesses exist to provide this access.

# › Review Questions

## Concepts

1. What are smart buildings and smart transportation, along with other sensors to help people, considered?

   (A) Sensor networks
   (B) Assistive technologies
   (C) Intrusive technologies
   (D) Scalable solutions

2. What is an example of sharing images and allowing individuals to scan them for certain features?

   (A) Heuristics
   (B) Moore's law
   (C) Citizen science
   (D) Contaminated research

3. What is the name for programming code that is available to anyone to use or modify?

   (A) Licensed software
   (B) Open source software
   (C) Compiled software
   (D) Executable only software

4. What has Creative Commons provided?

   (A) Free use of other people's work
   (B) Illegal ways to share other people's creations
   (C) Licensing options by the owners of artifacts
   (D) Cooperative copyright arbitration

5. People trading personal information for perks from companies is an example of what?

   (A) The use of proxy servers
   (B) Privacy concerns
   (C) Legal issues
   (D) Authentication exposure

6. What is the term for showing someone information based on their prior searches and purchases?

   (A) Targeting advertising
   (B) Open source marketing
   (C) GPS marketing
   (D) Aggregation of data

7. Determining the credibility of online sources requires evaluating what credentials?

   (A) Author
   (B) Publisher
   (C) Site owner
   (D) All of the above

## Application of Concepts

8. How can the Internet help education?

   1. Online courses
   2. Online homework help sites
   3. Sites where students can post videos asking for immediate feedback

   (A) 1 and 2
   (B) 1 and 3
   (C) 2 and 3
   (D) All of the above

9. A business's website tracks items that are viewed by visitors to its site. Which question *cannot* be answered by tracking this data?

   (A) Which items will sell during each season in different parts of the world
   (B) The trending colors that could be popular in the next year
   (C) The income range of prospective customers
   (D) How many of each item to produce

10. Which of the following is an example of plagiarism?

    1. Writing about an idea you read about
    2. Making minor changes to wording in a paragraph
    3. Retyping text rather than copying and pasting it into a document

    (A) 1 and 2
    (B) 1 and 3
    (C) 2 and 3
    (D) All of the above

## ≫ Answers and Explanations

1. **B**—Smart buildings and smart transportation along with other sensors that help people can be considered assistive technology.

2. **C**—Sharing images and allowing individuals to scan them for certain features is an example of citizen science.

3. **B**—Open source software is available to anyone to use or modify.

4. **C**—Creative commons allow the owner to designate licensing options.

5. **B**—People trading personal information for perks from companies is an example of a privacy concern.

6. **A**—Targeted advertising is showing someone information based on their prior searches and purchases.

7. **D**—Determining the credibility of online sources requires evaluating the credentials of the author, publisher, and site owner.

8. **A**—Both online courses and online homework help sites currently exist. They can help students take courses not offered at their school and get help in the evenings and weekends. Posting videos with questions is not an effective way to get help.

9. **C**—The data tracked can provide reasonable information about everything except a potential customer's income level.

10. **D**—All of the examples are instances of plagiarism. Ideas must be cited as well as text that is only minimally changed and content you copy either by retyping or pasting into a document.

# › Rapid Review

Advances in technology have enabled the development of new and innovative creations and solutions in many fields. These advances have changed the way people interact with each other, in both positive and negative ways.

Positive changes include new assistive devices so those needing extra help can be more independent. Sensors are used to create smart buildings to save energy and smart transportation options to manage resources. There are also many new ways to communicate, including email, texting, and social media sites. These sites have also been instrumental in sharing information with a much wider audience than could have been previously reached through non-technology-related methods.

Technological advances have also enabled easy and even real-time collaboration to create documents. Having data sets online and accessible to the public helps share information and provides everyone the ability to search, or "mine," it for trends and patterns that could lead to the identification of new issues and opportunities. This data also enables "machine learning" that can lead to advances in a variety of fields, including medicine, entertainment, sports, and business.

Finding needed data in available databases is an important skill to learn. Search tools that use keywords and Boolean logic can help filter the data to better select the information needed from the database. An important digital literacy skill is the evaluation of websites to determine if the information in them is credible. Plagiarism is easy to do using the Internet by copying and pasting information without citing the owner of the information. However, it is equally easy to test for plagiarism.

New technological tools, such as GPS, take advantage of satellites to provide new ways to navigate during trips, and find restaurants, shopping, gas stations, and other locations along the way. These tools can also help find alternate routes to take in the event of traffic congestion or just for fun.

The use of "citizen scientists" to aid in research and storing or processing digital data is an example of crowdsourcing. Citizen scientists are useful to research teams that have limited time, funding, or members to collect the wide variety or volume of data needed for better analysis and problem-solving.

The development of the Creative Commons licensing levels helps people share their creations and allow their reuse for specific uses with a wider audience. The tracking of their use and enforcement can be difficult and leads to issues about intellectual property and copyright. The Digital Millennium Copyright Act (DMCA) was created to help deal with protecting all digital creations—although we hear of it most often with cases of music and movies.

Illegal sharing of digital files is one of the downsides of new technologies. Illegal sharing is usually done through peer-to-peer networks. The unauthorized use or sharing of our personal data is also a major concern that impacts all of us. Aggregating data to remove the ability to identify an individual's personal data will remain a concern since it is dependent on the abilities of the person or team doing the aggregating to fully understand and implement a complete masking process.

Similarly, the tracking of people through their apps, photos, and browsing history is a privacy and security concern. Tied in with this, advertisers use targeted ads based on places we go and sites we visit. People often willingly provide this information to receive benefits such as discount coupons.

We must remain aware of the digital divide that separates those with access to the Internet from those who do not—whether it's due to being in a more remote location or lack of funds to pay for Internet service or devices. Remember too, that some governments monitor and block certain users and sites on the Internet, usually those critical of the country's leadership.

STEP **5**

# Build Your Test-Taking Confidence

AP Computer Science Principles Practice Exam 1

AP Computer Science Principles Practice Exam 2

# AP Computer Science Principles: Practice Exam 1

## Multiple-Choice Questions
### ANSWER SHEET

| | | |
|---|---|---|
| 1 Ⓐ Ⓑ Ⓒ Ⓓ | 26 Ⓐ Ⓑ Ⓒ Ⓓ | 51 Ⓐ Ⓑ Ⓒ Ⓓ |
| 2 Ⓐ Ⓑ Ⓒ Ⓓ | 27 Ⓐ Ⓑ Ⓒ Ⓓ | 52 Ⓐ Ⓑ Ⓒ Ⓓ |
| 3 Ⓐ Ⓑ Ⓒ Ⓓ | 28 Ⓐ Ⓑ Ⓒ Ⓓ | 53 Ⓐ Ⓑ Ⓒ Ⓓ |
| 4 Ⓐ Ⓑ Ⓒ Ⓓ | 29 Ⓐ Ⓑ Ⓒ Ⓓ | 54 Ⓐ Ⓑ Ⓒ Ⓓ |
| 5 Ⓐ Ⓑ Ⓒ Ⓓ | 30 Ⓐ Ⓑ Ⓒ Ⓓ | 55 Ⓐ Ⓑ Ⓒ Ⓓ |
| 6 Ⓐ Ⓑ Ⓒ Ⓓ | 31 Ⓐ Ⓑ Ⓒ Ⓓ | 56 Ⓐ Ⓑ Ⓒ Ⓓ |
| 7 Ⓐ Ⓑ Ⓒ Ⓓ | 32 Ⓐ Ⓑ Ⓒ Ⓓ | 57 Ⓐ Ⓑ Ⓒ Ⓓ |
| 8 Ⓐ Ⓑ Ⓒ Ⓓ | 33 Ⓐ Ⓑ Ⓒ Ⓓ | 58 Ⓐ Ⓑ Ⓒ Ⓓ |
| 9 Ⓐ Ⓑ Ⓒ Ⓓ | 34 Ⓐ Ⓑ Ⓒ Ⓓ | 59 Ⓐ Ⓑ Ⓒ Ⓓ |
| 10 Ⓐ Ⓑ Ⓒ Ⓓ | 35 Ⓐ Ⓑ Ⓒ Ⓓ | 60 Ⓐ Ⓑ Ⓒ Ⓓ |
| 11 Ⓐ Ⓑ Ⓒ Ⓓ | 36 Ⓐ Ⓑ Ⓒ Ⓓ | 61 Ⓐ Ⓑ Ⓒ Ⓓ |
| 12 Ⓐ Ⓑ Ⓒ Ⓓ | 37 Ⓐ Ⓑ Ⓒ Ⓓ | 62 Ⓐ Ⓑ Ⓒ Ⓓ |
| 13 Ⓐ Ⓑ Ⓒ Ⓓ | 38 Ⓐ Ⓑ Ⓒ Ⓓ | 63 Ⓐ Ⓑ Ⓒ Ⓓ |
| 14 Ⓐ Ⓑ Ⓒ Ⓓ | 39 Ⓐ Ⓑ Ⓒ Ⓓ | 64 Ⓐ Ⓑ Ⓒ Ⓓ |
| 15 Ⓐ Ⓑ Ⓒ Ⓓ | 40 Ⓐ Ⓑ Ⓒ Ⓓ | 65 Ⓐ Ⓑ Ⓒ Ⓓ |
| 16 Ⓐ Ⓑ Ⓒ Ⓓ | 41 Ⓐ Ⓑ Ⓒ Ⓓ | 66 Ⓐ Ⓑ Ⓒ Ⓓ |
| 17 Ⓐ Ⓑ Ⓒ Ⓓ | 42 Ⓐ Ⓑ Ⓒ Ⓓ | 67 Ⓐ Ⓑ Ⓒ Ⓓ |
| 18 Ⓐ Ⓑ Ⓒ Ⓓ | 43 Ⓐ Ⓑ Ⓒ Ⓓ | 68 Ⓐ Ⓑ Ⓒ Ⓓ |
| 19 Ⓐ Ⓑ Ⓒ Ⓓ | 44 Ⓐ Ⓑ Ⓒ Ⓓ | 69 Ⓐ Ⓑ Ⓒ Ⓓ |
| 20 Ⓐ Ⓑ Ⓒ Ⓓ | 45 Ⓐ Ⓑ Ⓒ Ⓓ | 70 Ⓐ Ⓑ Ⓒ Ⓓ |
| 21 Ⓐ Ⓑ Ⓒ Ⓓ | 46 Ⓐ Ⓑ Ⓒ Ⓓ | 71 Ⓐ Ⓑ Ⓒ Ⓓ |
| 22 Ⓐ Ⓑ Ⓒ Ⓓ | 47 Ⓐ Ⓑ Ⓒ Ⓓ | 72 Ⓐ Ⓑ Ⓒ Ⓓ |
| 23 Ⓐ Ⓑ Ⓒ Ⓓ | 48 Ⓐ Ⓑ Ⓒ Ⓓ | 73 Ⓐ Ⓑ Ⓒ Ⓓ |
| 24 Ⓐ Ⓑ Ⓒ Ⓓ | 49 Ⓐ Ⓑ Ⓒ Ⓓ | 74 Ⓐ Ⓑ Ⓒ Ⓓ |
| 25 Ⓐ Ⓑ Ⓒ Ⓓ | 50 Ⓐ Ⓑ Ⓒ Ⓓ | |

# AP Computer Science Principles: Practice Exam 1

## Multiple-Choice Questions

Time: 2 hours
Number of questions: 74
The multiple-choice questions represent 60% of your total score.

Directions: Choose the one best answer for each question. Some questions at the end of the test have more than one correct answer; for these, you will be instructed to choose two answer choices.

Tear out the answer sheet on the previous page and grid in your answers using a pencil.

Consider how much time you have left before spending too much time on any one problem.

---

**AP Computer Science Principles Exam Reference Sheet**

On the AP Computer Science Principles Exam, you will be given a reference sheet to use while you're taking the multiple-choice test. A copy of this seven-page reference sheet is included in the Appendix of this book (reprinted by permission from the College Board).

To make taking this practice test like taking the actual exam, you should tear out the reference sheet so you can easily refer to it while taking the test. Save these reference pages since you'll need to use them when you take AP Computer Science Principles Practice Exam 2.

If you lose the pages, the reference sheet is also available near the end of the PDF publication, "Assessment Overview and Performance Task Directions for Students" on the College Board Website. Here is the URL:

https://apcentral.collegeboard.org/pdf/ap-csp-student-task-directions.
    pdf?course=ap-computer-science-principles

---

GO ON TO THE NEXT PAGE

1. You won the lottery and elected to receive a lump sum! The largest number the bank's computer can store is $2^{31} - 1$ or 2,147,483,647. After depositing your lottery winnings of $2,500,000,000.00, what will the result be?

   (A) Your winnings were more than the largest number the bank's computers could hold, so an overflow error will occur.
   (B) Since decimal numbers are stored imprecisely in computers, a rounding error will occur.
   (C) The amount will be represented in machine code format, so converting it to decimal will show the balance in a more readable format.
   (D) The amount will be represented in hexadecimal, so converting it to decimal will make the balance more readable.

2. You stop by and purchase your favorite snack after school one day. You notice the cash register shows the change you are owed as: $0.04999999 rather than $0.05. How is this possible?

   (A) The cash register DISPLAY procedure has an error.
   (B) Since decimal numbers are stored imprecisely in computers, a rounding error occurred.
   (C) It's displaying the change owed in a different currency.
   (D) The amount is represented in hexadecimal rather than decimal. Alert the store clerk to make the conversion to decimal.

3. You are assigned a parking space in a large parking lot by an automated machine. You recognize that the parking space number is displayed in binary, but the parking spots are labeled in decimal numbers. Convert the parking space number 10011011 to decimal to know where to park and avoid getting towed.

   (A) 154
   (B) 155
   (C) 157
   (D) 9F

4. When designing a web page, you see a color you want to use listed in hexadecimal as #50C878. Which color is it, given the decimal equivalents (Red, Green, Blue)?

   (A) (32, 76, 414)
   (B) (50, 118, 78)
   (C) (80, 200, 120)
   (D) (128, 310, 170)

5. You are designing a UI (user interface) for use by multiple international travelers. How can you best communicate the options and features of the software program so most people can understand them?

   (A) Write the UI in Spanish and Chinese, two of the most common languages spoken worldwide.
   (B) Use an API to interface with a translation website for those who need it.
   (C) Provide a link to an online dictionary so words users do not know can be quickly looked up.
   (D) Use images to represent features of the program.

6. The principal hired the programming class to write a program to reserve parking spots in the student parking lot. She wants seniors to have the best spots. What is the best way the programming class can verify a student is a senior?

   (A) The program can loop through the school district rosters for every student name.
   (B) Grade can be an input field that is then passed to the procedure to select an available spot.
   (C) Use an API to integrate with the school's information system hosted off-site to check grade level.
   (D) Have students upload a photo from the school registrar showing their school grade with their parking spot request.

GO ON TO THE NEXT PAGE

7. You have to change a program written a year ago by someone else. A sample section of code is below. How could the original program author have helped someone making changes at a later date?

```
PROCEDURE a(x, y, z)
    IF x < y
    {
        x ← z
    }
```

(A) Provided the original program requirements
(B) Added a video describing the program design and functionality
(C) Used procedure and variable names that described their purpose and content
(D) Provided written documentation of the application development process

**Questions 8–9 are based on the code below. Assume all lists and variables have been properly initialized.**

8. What does the code do?

(A) Plays a song from the playlist.
(B) If a song requested by the user is in the playlist, plays it; otherwise adds it to the end of the playlist and then plays it.
(C) Moves a song from its current position in the playlist to the end of it, then plays the next one in the list.
(D) Identifies songs the user wants to hear, but does not own. Provides a way to purchase the song and appends it to their playlist.

9. In the code, if "play" is a procedure, what does "song" represent in the line: play(song)?

(A) It is the name of the procedure for documentation purposes.
(B) It is an input value where the user requests the song to be played.

(C) It is a value being passed to the procedure via an argument that will be used as a parameter in the procedure.
(D) It is an expression that must be evaluated to be used in the procedure.

10. Which statement is NOT true?

(A) Lower-level languages are easier to debug because the language is closest to what the computer executes.
(B) Higher-level languages are easier to debug because the language is closer to natural language.
(C) Lower-level languages provide less abstraction.
(D) Higher-level languages are easier for people to code in because they are more like natural language.

11. If a simulation of the solar eclipse is set up to test the effectiveness of glasses to safely view the sun, which scenario below is most likely if the first test shows the glasses are inadequate?

(A) The team can modify the degree of darkness and retest quickly to determine the threshold of effectiveness.
(B) The team should stop the test and notify the company that makes the glasses.
(C) The team should rerun the test multiple times to ensure the results are valid.
(D) The team should rewrite the code for the simulation, and then retest.

GO ON TO THE NEXT PAGE

12. A simulation of conditions for a new sensor to be used with self-driving cars is being designed. The pseudo-code for the test is below.

```
When car starts, turn sensor on and
set incident_counter to 0
When detect object 3 feet or closer,
redirect steering wheel away from
object
Add one to incident_counter
```

Which conditions should the simulation test about the sensor?

(A) If the incident_counter > 10, then the sensor is successful.
(B) If the incident_counter is 0, then the sensor is successful.
(C) Set up objects at 3 feet, less than 3 feet, and greater than 3 feet to determine the action taken.
(D) If the car avoids an accident, then the sensor is successful.

13. A series of binary numbers appears on your computer screen. What do they represent?

(A) The source code for the program after compilation.
(B) The machine instruction that caused the error.
(C) The error message before converting it to words using the ASCII table.
(D) It is impossible to tell the representation without knowing the context of their use.

14. Which of the following will evaluate to "true"?

 i. (true AND true) OR (true AND false)
 ii. NOT(true OR false)
 iii. NOT(false) AND NOT(true AND false)

(A) i and ii
(B) i and iii
(C) ii and iii
(D) i, ii, and iii

15. What outcome will the Boolean conditions in the diagram produce at steps 1, 2, and 3?

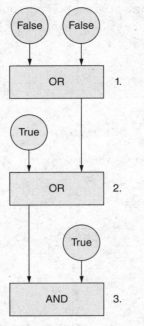

(A) 1-True, 2-True, 3-True
(B) 1-False, 2-False, 3-True
(C) 1-False, 2-True, 3-True
(D) 1-True, 2-False, 3-False

16. A camera watching an eagle's nest starts recording when a motion detector starts. Which of the following is metadata?

(A) The latitude and longitude of the nest
(B) The date and time the motion is detected
(C) The number of eagles using the nest
(D) The number of frames per second the camera records

17. Susie's mother wants a copy of a photo from a family vacation that Susie took. The picture is too large to email. How should Susie compress the image if her mother wants to print a large copy of it suitable for framing?

(A) She should use a lossless compression technique, which will be needed to print a version with high enough quality to frame.
(B) She should use a lossy compression technique to obtain enough compression to send the image.
(C) They should be combined for the best compression technique.
(D) Any compression technique will be sufficient in this case.

GO ON TO THE NEXT PAGE

18. When listening to an online music service, you request songs "like" a specific song. How does the music site determine what to play?

    (A) It plays songs you have played previously.
    (B) It plays the most requested songs from all listeners.
    (C) It uses data-mining techniques to determine patterns in the music that are similar.
    (D) It plays a random selection.

19. Which one of the following would be a good project for citizen scientists and why?

    (A) Counting pine trees in urban conditions to get accurate data about the spread of the pine beetle
    (B) Identifying new stars using personal telescopes to keep costs lower for the tracking organization
    (C) Reading different genre books and evaluating them so book publishers know which types of book manuscripts to accept and market
    (D) Counting fish in a lake to know if the fish are safe to consume

20. What describes the process of searching data sets for incomplete data records to process?

    (A) Classifying
    (B) Cleaning
    (C) Clustering
    (D) Filtering

21. A teacher wants to determine student opinions of computer science before and after taking a course. She gives students a survey on the first and last days of class. The survey includes questions about students' impressions about computer science, if the teacher communicated effectively, if the teacher was positive about the course material, and if students gave their best effort in the course. What questions can be determined from the survey data?

    i. If students who moved from a negative to positive impression of computer science after taking the course also thought the teacher communicated effectively
    ii. Which students plan to major in computer science after taking the course
    iii. If the students who did not change their existing view of computer science after taking the course gave their best effort in the course

    (A) i
    (B) i and iii
    (C) ii and iii
    (D) i, ii, and iii

22. Given the table of data about car accidents, which outcome is supported by the data?

    (A) Drivers ages 16–25 have the fewest accidents.
    (B) More accidents occur on the weekdays.
    (C) Drivers age 26–50 have fewer accidents than the other two age groups.
    (D) Adult drivers have more accidents on weekdays during rush hour.

| Most common type of accident | Number of accidents by 16–25 yr. old drivers | Number of accidents by 26–50 yr. old drivers | Number of accidents by 51–100 yr. old drivers | Total number of accidents | Accident occurred on weekday | Accident occurred on weekend |
|---|---|---|---|---|---|---|
| Rear-end collision | 311 | 211 | 250 | 772 | 257 | 515 |
| Ran light at intersection | 215 | 121 | 152 | 488 | 191 | 297 |
| Ran stop sign | 182 | 87 | 92 | 361 | 177 | 184 |

GO ON TO THE NEXT PAGE

23. Which of the following is an example where analysis of large data sets would NOT be able to identify potentially valuable information?

   (A) Identifying risk factors for certain health issues
   (B) Identifying which aspects banks should focus on to minimize loan defaults
   (C) Enabling companies to know when to schedule replacement of equipment parts because of usage and increased maintenance on them
   (D) Enabling businesses to know what to produce and when for maximum sales

24. Why do businesses and scientists attempt to analyze big data?

   (A) To gain insights smaller subsets of data may not provide
   (B) To confirm findings from smaller data sets
   (C) To identify potential problems in the metadata
   (D) To obtain economies of scale with hardware needed to store the data based on Moore's law

25. How do the World Wide Web and the Internet work together?

   (A) They perform the same functionality.
   (B) The Web uses HTTP to share computational artifacts using the Internet.
   (C) The Internet uses the Web to connect devices to share data.
   (D) The Internet has the "deep" net and "dark" net but the Web does not.

26. If a fire occurs at a major Internet hub, what is the result?

   (A) Internet traffic will be routed to its destination a different way because of the redundancy built into the Internet.
   (B) The part of the globe that is served by that Internet hub will be down because of the end-to-end architecture of the Internet.
   (C) Different IP addresses will be assigned to devices that were impacted by the unavailability of the Internet hub.
   (D) People can use dedicated phone lines as a backup with no change in service.

27. In the following web address, how many domain levels are there?
http://anytime.anyway.anyplace.edu/lessons/notes/apex.docx

   (A) 6
   (B) 5
   (C) 4
   (D) 3

28. If a company is trying to determine whether to upgrade its bandwidth based on the following graph, what should they measure?

   (A) Amount of data uploaded as it includes strategic company backup data
   (B) Amount of data downloaded as it has the largest impact on the bandwidth
   (C) Frequency of the peak times
   (D) Type of devices employees use on the network

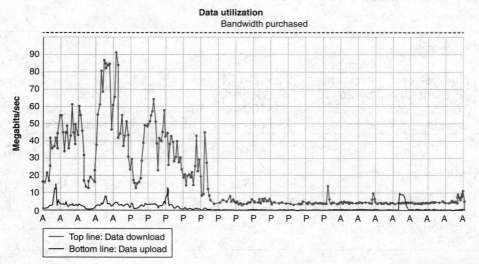

29. Why is the trust model of the Internet important?

    (A) It ensures the private security key has not been compromised.

    (B) It establishes a dedicated line between two destinations to ensure security.

    (C) It enables the secure transfer of data, such as a credit card transaction, which allows online purchasing.

    (D) It ensures the privacy of customers making online transactions

30. What happens in a DDoS attack?

    (A) Bots search for malware-detecting software that is out of date and prevents the uploading of new versions without the owner knowing.

    (B) Firewalls are deactivated so malware can enter the network.

    (C) The targeted site is flooded with too many false requests and crashes.

    (D) Sensitive data is not encrypted before being transmitted over the Internet making it vulnerable to interception.

31. Which option below is a potential negative result of storing data in the cloud?

    (A) You have to rely on someone else to maintain the security of the data.

    (B) Online collaboration could result in accidentally overwriting someone's changes to a document.

    (C) You must store duplicates of data stored in the cloud in case you cannot access your data when needed.

    (D) The company storing your data could hold it for ransom until you paid extra fees.

32. If an organization wants to change its website name from .org to .edu, what do they need to do to ensure they can still be found on the Web?

    (A) Register the new name with a DNS (Domain Name System) site.

    (B) The organization can start using the new name immediately since only the top-level domain changed.

    (C) Notify IETF, the organization that maintains names on the Internet.

    (D) Post the new name on the organization's website up to 10 days prior to the switchover.

33. Which of the following is true about packets?

    (A) The receiving device acknowledges the first and last packets to indicate receipt of the data stream.

    (B) Packets travel in order to their destination.

    (C) Packets follow the shortest path to their destination.

    (D) Packets are reassembled at their final destination.

34. How do TCP and IP interact?

    (A) IP forwards the data to the DNS server to identify which TCP to use.

    (B) TCP hands off control to HTTP, which passes it to IP.

    (C) TCP creates packets from the data to be sent and transfers control to IP for routing. TCP then reassembles the packets at the destination.

    (D) IP uses the SSL in conjunction with TCP to securely send data.

35. Data mining allows organizations to process huge data sets to find new patterns, connections, or opportunities. Which of the following is NOT a downside of data mining?

    (A) It may require having to train staff and allocate resources based on data results.

    (B) More relevant information is included on the company's website.

    (C) It is expensive to collect, store, and process data.

    (D) It is risky for decision making if the data is interpreted incorrectly.

36. Computers have enabled new innovations in a variety of industries. In the entertainment business it has become much easier to purchase and share new music. What concern has been raised as a result?

    (A) People are modifying other people's content and claiming the Creative Commons licensing allows it.

    (B) People are being discovered for their music because others are posting it to music-sharing sites.

    (C) People are sharing content without the author/owner's permission.

    (D) Artists are adding their music to streaming services with Creative Commons licensing.

GO ON TO THE NEXT PAGE

**37.** Which of following are legal and ethical concerns because of DMCA?

(A) Peer-to-peer networks used for illegal file sharing

(B) Music and movie downloads and streaming services not charging enough for their services

(C) Licensing stipulations that allow incorporating music into other artforms

(D) Controlled intellectual property sharing

**38.** What is a benefit of the government posting databases for public use?

(A) It is a way to identify the need for new policies and regulations.

(B) Consumers can learn more about how their individual data is being collected, stored, and used.

(C) Companies can opt out to prevent competitors from learning about their business.

(D) All businesses can access the data at no cost, aiding those businesses that would otherwise not have the resources to obtain the data on their own.

**39.** Which algorithm will display the smallest number in a list of positive numbers? Assume Max is a variable holding the largest number in the list.

(A)
```
smallest ← -1
FOR EACH num IN list
{
        IF (smallest < num)
        {
            smallest ← num
        }
}
DISPLAY (smallest)
```
(B)
```
smallest ← Max
FOR EACH num IN list
{
        IF (smallest > num)
        {
            smallest ← num
        }
}
DISPLAY (smallest)
```
(C)
```
smallest ← -1
FOR EACH num IN list
{
        IF (smallest > num)
        {
            smallest ← num
        }
}
DISPLAY (smallest)
```
(D)
```
smallest ← Max
FOR EACH num IN list
{
        IF (smallest < num)
        {
            smallest ← num
        }
}
DISPLAY (smallest)
```

**40.** For a binary search to produce accurate results, what must be true of the data?

(A) The data must be unsorted.

(B) The data must be sorted.

(C) The data must not have duplicates.

(D) The data must be fewer than a billion records. Otherwise the search requires too many resources for processing.

**41.** Which of these is a Boolean expression?

(A) `X ← 57`

(B) `Y ← temp * 120 / 100`

(C) `(temp > 32)`

(D) `72 + 12 - (12 * 6) → z`

**42.** What can be determined from the following program flow?

```
Intro()
Rules()
Play()
Score()
DISPLAY (HighScore())
```

(A) A game is played by calling different procedures.

(B) An error will occur due to invalid procedure names.

(C) Parameters are missing from the procedures resulting in a runtime error.

(D) A compile time error occurs due to Score() and HighScore().

**43.** Which statement's format is incorrect?

(A)
```
IF (NOT (x > y))
{
        DISPLAY(message)
}
```
(B) `x ← x + y`

(C) `list[i] ← list[j]`

(D)
```
ELSE
    DISPLAY(new message)
```

GO ON TO THE NEXT PAGE

**44.** Which algorithm should be used to find a phone number on a contact list?

I.
Sort the contact list by name
Search for the phone number using a binary search
Display the correct phone number

II.
Sort the contact list by area code
Search for the phone number using a linear search
Display the correct phone number

(A) I
(B) II
(C) I and II are equally effective.
(D) A combination of both I and II should be used.

**45.** Why does a computer playing chess use a heuristic algorithm?

(A) It ensures the computer only wins a certain number of times making it a more enjoyable experience for people.
(B) It ensures humans only win a certain percentage based on statistics.
(C) It takes too long to analyze all possible moves, so the computer takes the next best move.
(D) It checks each possible combination of moves for the best move.

**46.** What does iteration with computer science loops mean?

(A) Executing code once
(B) Repeating a block of code until a condition is met
(C) Duplicating a section of code multiple times in a program
(D) Identifying the error condition

**47.** If a list named **snacks** contains the values:

```
snacks ← ["chocolate", "peanuts",
"granola", "chips", "grapes"]
A variable place is assigned the
value:
place ← LENGTH(snacks)
```

What will the value snacks[place] contain?
(A) 5, the number of items in the list
(B) 6, the number of letters in the word "grapes"
(C) grapes, which is the value in the 5th position of the list
(D) Error, a list cannot be accessed in this way.

**48.** Will both of the following two blocks produce correct results? Assume all variables have been properly initialized.

(A) Only Block 1 is correct.
(B) Only Block 2 is correct.
(C) Both blocks are correct.
(D) Neither block is correct.

```
Block 1

IF (temp ≥ 80)
{
    hotDay ← hotDay + 1
}
ELSE IF (temp ≥ 60)
{
    perfectDay ← perfectDay + 1
}
ELSE
{
    coldDay ← coldDay + 1
{
```

```
Block 2

IF (temp ≤ 80)
{
    perfectDay ← perfectDay + 1
}
ELSE IF (temp ≤ 60)
{
    coldDay ← coldDay + 1
}
ELSE
{
    hotDay ← hotDay + 1
}
```

GO ON TO THE NEXT PAGE

**49.** Determining that an algorithm is intractable means it runs in:

(A) an acceptable amount of time even for large data sets.
(B) less time for worst-case scenarios than average scenarios.
(C) an exponential amount of time possibly even for small data sets making it unable to run for large data sets.
(D) a fractional amount of time for fractional values.

**50.** Which order has the programming languages in most abstract to least abstract order?

(A) Text-based language, assembly language, block-based language, machine language
(B) Block-based language, text-based language, machine language, assembly language
(C) Machine language, assembly language, block-based language, text-based language
(D) Block-based language, text-based language, assembly language, machine language

**51.** Which type of programming statement includes Boolean conditions to determine the section of code to execute?

(A) Functions
(B) Complex
(C) Selection
(D) Contrasting

**52.** Which set of code will calculate the letter grade correctly? Assume the average is a variable holding the student average.

(A)
```
IF (average > 59)
{
    grade ← D
}
    ELSE
    {
        IF (grade > 69)
        {
            grade ← C
        }
        ELSE
        {
            IF (grade > 79)
            {
                grade ← B
            }
            ELSE
            {
                    IF (grade > 89)
                    {
                        grade ← A
                    }
                    ELSE
                    {
                        grade ← F
                    }
            }
        }
    }
```

(B)
```
IF (average < 59)
{
    grade ← D
}
ELSE
{
    IF (grade < 69)
    {
        grade ← C
    }
    ELSE
    {
        IF (grade < 79)
        {
            grade ← B
        }
        ELSE
        {
            IF (grade < 89)
            {
                grade ← A
            }
            ELSE
            {
                grade ← F
            }
        }
    }
}
```

GO ON TO THE NEXT PAGE

(C)
```
IF (average > 90)
{
    grade ← A
}
ELSE
{
    IF (grade > 80)
    {
        grade ← B
    }
    ELSE
    {
        IF (grade < 70)
        {
            grade ← C
        }
        ELSE
        {
            IF (grade < 60)
            {
                grade ← D
            }
            ELSE
            {
                grade ← F
            }
        }
    }
}
```

(D)
```
IF (average > 89)
{
    grade ← A
}
ELSE
{
    IF (grade > 79)
    {
        grade ← B
    }
    ELSE
    {
        IF (grade < 69)
        {
            grade ← C
        }
        ELSE
        {
            IF (grade < 59)
            {
                grade ← D
            }
            ELSE
            {
                grade ← F
            }
        }
    }
}
```

**53.** The code below is a robot algorithm. Which diagram matches the code?

```
MOVE_FORWARD()
MOVE_FORWARD()
ROTATE_LEFT()
MOVE_FORWARD()
MOVE_FORWARD()
ROTATE_RIGHT()
MOVE_FORWARD()
ROTATE_LEFT()
```

(A)

(B)

(C)

(D)

GO ON TO THE NEXT PAGE

**54.** What benefit does an API provide?

(A) It allows programmers to share their code via the API for others to test.

(B) It connects software components providing pre-written and tested code available for use.

(C) It provides algorithms for difficult code to be reviewed.

(D) It provides documentation programmers can use for their programs rather than creating their own.

**55.** What is the value of *x* after the code below runs?

```
PROCEDURE calcTemp (temp)
{
    newTemp ← (5/9 * (temp - 32))
    RETURN (newTemp)
}

x ← calcTemp(50)
```

(A) −10
(B) 10
(C) 4
(D) −4

**56.** What is the value of *y* after the following statements?

```
x ← 10
x ← x + 4
y ← x MOD 3
```

(A) 0
(B) 2
(C) 3
(D) 4

**57.** What is displayed after the following code runs?

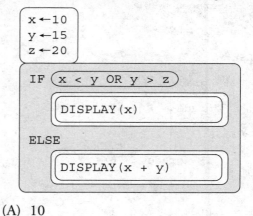

(A) 10
(B) 15
(C) 20
(D) 25

**58.** Which of the following two algorithms produces the sum of the elements in the list? Assume the list is initialized and is not empty.

(A) Block 1
(B) Block 2
(C) Blocks 1 and 2
(D) Neither Block 1 nor 2

**Block 1**

```
x   ← 1
sum ← 0
REPEAT LENGTH(list) TIMES
{
    sum ← sum + (x)
    x ← x + 1
}
DISPLAY("The total is: ", sum)
```

**Block 2**

```
x   ← LENGTH(list)
sum ← 0
REPEAT x TIMES
{
    sum ← sum + list[x]
    x ← x - 1
}
DISPLAY("The total is: ", sum)
```

GO ON TO THE NEXT PAGE

**59.** What will the following code produce?

```
x ← 5
y ← x
x ← y + 5

REPEAT UNTIL x > y
{
        DISPLAY ("Hello World!")
}
```

(A) "Hello World!" will be printed multiple times.
(B) The code inside the REPEAT UNTIL loop never executes.
(C) The REPEAT UNTIL loop never ends, creating an infinite loop.
(D) The program will have a runtime error.

**Questions 60–62 refer to the following code.**

```
snacks ← ["popcorn", "candy", "grapes",
"apples"]
FOR EACH snack IN snacks
{
    IF NOT(snack = "banana")
    {
            APPEND(snacks, "banana")
    }
    DISPLAY snack
}
```

**60.** What will the code display?

(A) popcorn, candy, grapes, apples, banana
(B) popcorn, candy, grapes, apples, banana, banana
(C) popcorn, candy, grapes, apples, banana, banana, banana
(D) popcorn, candy, grapes, apples, banana, banana, banana, banana

**61.** What is the index position of apples?

(A) 3
(B) 4
(C) 5
(D) 6

**62.** What is the value of snacks after the following code is run?

```
snacks ← ["donut", "french fries",
"candy", "popcorn", "candy", "grapes",
"apples", "banana"]
j ← 1
REPEAT UNTIL j = 5
{
    snacks[j] ← [j + 4]
    j ← j + 1
}
```

(A) 5, 6, 7, 8, candy, grapes, apples, banana
(B) popcorn, candy, grapes, apples, popcorn, candy, grapes, apples,
(C) popcorn, popcorn, popcorn, popcorn, candy, grapes, apples, banana
(D) popcorn, popcorn, popcorn, popcorn, popcorn, popcorn, popcorn, popcorn

**63.** What is displayed after the following code runs?

```
line1 = "Good luck"
line2 = " on the AP exam!"
DISPLAY (line1 + line2)
```

(A) Error message, cannot add text fields
(B) Good luck on the AP exam!
(C) Good luck
    on the AP exam!
(D) 24, which is the number of characters in the text fields

**64.** What is an iterative software development process designed to do?

(A) To produce better software with a proven process
(B) To shorten the time of developing software by beginning to code while the requirements are being determined
(C) To eliminate the testing step by using only APIs
(D) To develop it right the first time through the iterative process

GO ON TO THE NEXT PAGE

**65.** The programmer tests an app she wrote using one set of test cases. Since the app was developed for her personal use, does it need to undergo further testing?

(A) Yes, all software should be tested with a variety of test cases to ensure the code works as expected.

(B) No, since the app is for personal use, less stringent testing is acceptable.

(C) Additional testing is required only when there are more than 25 lines of code

(D) Additional testing is needed when procedures are used.

**66.** Which set of code will move the robot from start to stop and end facing the correct direction? The robot may not move into gray blocks.

| | | | Stop ← | |
|---|---|---|---|---|
| | | | | |
| | | | | |
| | | | | |
| Start → | | | | |

(A)
```
MOVE_FORWARD()
MOVE_FORWARD()
MOVE_FORWARD()
ROTATE_LEFT()
MOVE_FORWARD()
ROTATE_RIGHT()
MOVE_FORWARD()
ROTATE_LEFT()
MOVE_FORWARD()
MOVE_FORWARD()
MOVE_FORWARD()
ROTATE_LEFT()
MOVE_FORWARD()
```

(B)
```
MOVE_FORWARD()
MOVE_FORWARD()
MOVE_FORWARD()
MOVE_FORWARD()
ROTATE_LEFT()
MOVE_FORWARD()
MOVE_FORWARD()
MOVE_FORWARD()
MOVE_FORWARD()
ROTATE_LEFT()
MOVE_FORWARD()
```

(C)
```
MOVE_FORWARD()
ROTATE_LEFT()
MOVE_FORWARD()
MOVE_FORWARD()
MOVE_FORWARD()
MOVE_FORWARD()
ROTATE_RIGHT()
MOVE_FORWARD()
MOVE_FORWARD()
```

(D)
```
MOVE_FORWARD()
MOVE_FORWARD()
MOVE_FORWARD()
ROTATE_RIGHT()
MOVE_FORWARD()
ROTATE_LEFT()
MOVE_FORWARD()
ROTATE_RIGHT()
MOVE_FORWARD()
MOVE_FORWARD()
MOVE_FORWARD()
ROTATE_RIGHT()
MOVE_FORWARD()
```

**67.** Cloud-based data storage is best when what conditions are true of those working with the data? Select two answers.

(A) They are in a secured location.

(B) They are in separate locations.

(C) They are dealing with sensitive data.

(D) They have limited storage at their location.

**68.** Data has been collected about medicine trial results. The privacy of those in the trial needs to be protected. Is data aggregation sufficient if the patient name is not used but zip code, doctor name, and pharmacy are used and the data is password protected? Select two answers.

(A) Yes, because a name is not associated with it.

(B) Yes, because the data is aggregated.

(C) No, because the zip code and pharmacy could be used to drill down to potentially identify patients in the trial.

(D) No, because the data filtering could still search for doctors involved in the trial and, if used with zip code, could identify potential participants.

GO ON TO THE NEXT PAGE

69. In putting together a team, the project manager wants to have scientists, gamers, artists, and computer scientists. What is the argument for creating this team? Select two answers.

    (A) It will help get budget money from each division.
    (B) Each can work independently on their part and then combine their work.
    (C) Collaboration efforts help save time and produce better results.
    (D) Different perspectives will help develop a better product.

70. Which two protocols are responsible for breaking the data into packets and putting it back together at the destination and routing the packets to their destination? Select two answers.

    (A) TCP
    (B) HTTP
    (C) FTP
    (D) IP

71. Why should public key encryption be used? Select two answers.

    (A) It is shorter than other ciphers.
    (B) It cannot be broken with brute force techniques.
    (C) It uses an asymmetric key making it harder to decrypt.
    (D) It uses a symmetric key making it harder to decrypt.

72. Which of the following can be stored in a bit? Select two answers.

    (A) The result of a number MOD 2
    (B) A Boolean variable
    (C) A variable that could hold a range of positive values
    (D) A computer that can be on, off, or in "sleep" mode

73. Sending data off-site is a disaster recovery backup strategy. Which concerns can occur from this strategy? Select two answers.

    (A) Security concerns if unencrypted data is transferred off-site on a regular basis
    (B) Privacy concerns if the data were intercepted and decrypted exposing personal data
    (C) Compatibility issues as computers and software change, the data may be unusable on newer systems
    (D) Compression issues with sending large quantities over the network to a server in a different location

74. How has cloud computing helped with communication? Select two answers.

    (A) By allowing asynchronous communication with email and text messaging
    (B) By allowing synchronous methods of communication such as video conferencing
    (C) By reducing the need for translation services since data can be quickly accessed from anywhere
    (D) By providing cloud-based presentation tools to use with local data

**STOP. End of Exam**

# AP Computer Science Principles: Practice Exam 1

## Answers and Explanations

1. **A**—The huge lottery winnings added to your previous balance were more than the largest integer the bank account could accommodate, so an overflow error occurred.

2. **B**—Floating point numbers, (e.g., numbers with fractions) are stored imprecisely in the computer and can cause rounding errors. This is why they should not be used for monetary transactions. The clerk owes you a nickel.

3. **B**—Take the binary number and create a table of the powers of 2, starting with $2^0$ in the rightmost position. For every column there is a 1 in the binary number, add the corresponding value of $2^x$.

| $2^7$ | $2^6$ | $2^5$ | $2^4$ | $2^3$ | $2^2$ | $2^1$ | $2^0$ |
|-----|-----|-----|-----|-----|-----|-----|-----|
| 128 | 64 | 32 | 16 | 8 | 4 | 2 | 1 |
| 1 | 0 | 0 | 1 | 1 | 0 | 1 | 1 |

$128 + 16 + 8 + 2 + 1 = 155_{10}$

4. **C**—You need to convert the number for each color from hexadecimal to decimal: 50 for Red, C8 for Green, 78 for Blue.

$50_{16} = 0101\ 0000_2$
Red:  $64 + 16 = 80$

$C8_{16} = 1100\ 1000_2$
Green: $128 + 64 + 8 = 200$

$78_{16} = 0111\ 1000_2$
Blue:  $64 + 32 + 16 + 8 = 120$

RGB (80, 200, 120)

5. **D**—The goal of the user interface is to provide a smooth and understandable experience. As an abstraction, images can provide the best way for users to understand the features of the software. If people do not speak the languages the software is using to display messages, then they may not understand that Google Translate and a dictionary are available options. Images provide the best option for this user interface.

6. **B**—Using a parameter with the procedure to indicate grade is the best solution. Due to security and privacy risks, the students should not integrate with the school system database. Adding a step to upload a photo is inefficient as is a loop to go through the district rosters each time.

7. **C**—Using well-named procedures and variable names makes code more readable and understandable. The original program requirements would not be useful as it may not have been updated as the program was modified. Similarly, a video may help to explain the original programmer's thought process, but it may be out of date and not very useful for understanding the code they wrote. Documenting the development process will not be useful to someone changing the code.

8. **B**—If the song the user typed is in the playlist, it will be played and a Boolean variable marked as true for ownership of the song. After checking all songs in the playlist, the song will be added to the playlist if it is not already there and then played.

9. **C**—When calling the procedure, play, the value passed to it is passed using an argument. It is a parameter when used internally in the procedure.

**10. A**— Lower-level languages are written in code closer to machine language. These are more difficult to debug for most people because the code is less like natural language.

**11. A**—A benefit of models and simulations is the ability to modify a variable and retest quickly. Running the test with the same values does not help the analysis. Running one test and then stopping is not an effective use of a simulation. Unless an error was identified, which it was not in this scenario, then rewriting the code will not determine if the glasses are effective to safely protect people's eyes.

**12. C**—Since the sensor is set to detect objects within 3 feet of it, the test should measure the sensor action at all of the boundary conditions.

**13. D**—A binary number can represent all types of data, but knowing the context for its use determines how it is interpreted. The software knows what the number represents at each point in the program and interprets it correctly.

**14. B**—The only time an AND condition is true is when both conditions are true. The only time an OR condition is true is when either or both conditions are true. Evaluating the conditions provided, only i and iii are true.

**15. C**—The only time an AND condition is true is when A and B are both true. The only time an OR condition is true is when either or both conditions are true. Evaluating the conditions in the diagram will produce the results in answer C.

**16. D**—Everything is data about the nest and the eagles using the nest except the number of frames the camera can record, which is data about the data, or metadata.

**17. A**—Only the lossless compression technique will allow the original uncompressed photo to be restored.

**18. C**—Data mining identifies patterns and correlations among the data. This will show similarities between songs to tag them as "like" others with comparable patterns for future selection.

**19. A**—Projects that are good for citizen scientists would be one where specialized equipment, such as a telescope or fish finder, would not be required and can be based on facts versus personal opinion. Counting trees would be the best use in this example.

**20. B**—Cleaning involves finding and either correcting or eliminating incomplete records. It also involves standardizing the data for the analysis to be performed. It could include removing some complete and correct data that is not needed for the planned analysis.

**21. B**—The survey results will show if students changed their mind in either direction or maintained their viewpoint about computer science if they felt the teacher communicated effectively and if they felt they gave their best effort. It will not show if students plan to major in computer science.

**22. C**—The data in the table shows that drivers in the 26–50 age bracket have the least number of accidents. The data cannot tell us when the drivers had an accident.

**23. D**—Analyzing big data can identify risk factors for all the issues except knowing exactly what consumers will purchase and when.

**24. A**—Smaller data sets may not have enough data to identify patterns or true trends. If a trend is noticed in a smaller data set, processing big data may not be necessary. It will not identify metadata issues, nor determine when hardware purchases should be made.

**25. B**—The World Wide Web is an application that uses HTTP to share documents, videos, images, and other files among devices connected to the Internet.

**26. A**—The redundancy designed into the Internet means data can be sent via different paths to reach its destination.

**27. C**—The domain levels go from the Top-Level Domain (.edu) to the left. Anyplace is the 2nd level, anyway is the 3rd level, and anytime is the 4th level.

28. **B**—Bandwidth measures the amount of data that can be transmitted in a specific amount of time. Therefore, knowing how much data needs to be downloaded on a regular basis is a key measurement as people generally download far more than they upload.

29. **C**—Certificate Authorities, or CAs, issue digital certificates to customers that confirm ownership of their encrypted keys with secure Internet communications. This enables us to have online shopping among other secure online transactions.

30. **C**—A Distributed Denial of Service attack floods a site with invalid requests, causing it to be unable to respond to legitimate requests.

31. **A**—Ensuring the security of your data is out of your control when you store it in the cloud.

32. **A**—The new name must be registered with a DNS site so the IP address will be associated with the new name and the site can be found. Your Internet Service Provider (ISP) can help with this or you can register it yourself.

33. **D**—Packets are created at the sending end of the transmission and reassembled at the final destination.

34. **C**—TCP creates packets and passes control of them to IP which routes them to their final destination. TCP then reassembles the packets to display.

35. **B**—Companies that take advantage of data mining can provide information that a majority of their customers want to see on their website. This is a benefit to the company and the consumer.

36. **C**—The ease in sharing digital files without the artist's permission is an ongoing concern in the music industry.

37. **A**—To protect intellectual property, the Digital Millennium Copyright Act (DMCA) works to prevent illegal file sharing, illegal movie and music downloads, and licensing violations. Peer-to-peer networks are often used to illegally share files of all types.

38. **D**—One of many benefits is that all businesses can access the data, making it easier for new businesses to have and analyze data the established businesses use.

39. **B**—This is the only option that will capture the smallest number in a list.

40. **B**—The data must be sorted for a binary search to work.

41. **C**—Booleans can only be true or false, and C is the only option that can evaluate to true or false.

42. **A**—The flow of procedures called indicate a game is being played. The procedure names and parameters are all correct.

43. **D**—You cannot have an ELSE statement without an IF statement.

44. **B**—The first algorithm sorts by name, but then uses a binary search using phone number. This may not return correct results. Therefore, option II using a linear search on a contact list sorted by area code will return the correct results and is more effective.

45. **C**—A heuristic is finding the best approximate solution when the actual solution is intractable. A computer checking all possible chess moves will slow the processing down, so a heuristic solution will improve the speed and the overall game experience for the player.

46. **B**—Iteration means "repeating," so a loop will repeat until a condition is met causing it to end.

47. **C**—Since place is 5, the length of the snacks list, snacks[place] refers to the element at the 5th position of the list, which is "grapes". List elements can be accessed using a constant, such as list[2] or a variable as in this example, list[place].

48. **A**—Block 1 produces correct results based on the temperature. Block 2 counts all temperatures ≤ 80 to be a perfectDay, rather than separating them by temperature. The IF condition is set up incorrectly.

49. **C**—Intractable algorithms do not run efficiently for large data sets.

50. **D**—Block-based languages are the closest to natural language and are the most abstract. Text-based language is next as it is also easy to read and use. Next is assembly language, which is less abstract and closer to machine language. Machine language is the least abstract and the hardest for people to work with.

51. **C**—Selection criteria filter data and only process those records that meet the criteria.

52. **D**—A causes any grade higher than 59 to be assigned the letter grade. B uses greater than rather than less than. C will be off by one. D is correct.

53. **D**—Only option D ends up in the correct block facing in the correct direction. Remember that ROTATE commands do not move the robot forward a block. They only change the direction in the current block the robot is in.

54. **B**—An API (Application Programming Interface) connects software modules making working programs available for use in other programs.

55. **B**—Follow the order of operations to determine the answer the code will return.

56. **B**—MOD calculations provide the remainder when the two numbers are divided.

57. **A**—An OR condition only needs one of the conditions to be true for the overall condition to be true. Since 10 is less than 15, the value of $x$ will be displayed.

58. **B**—Block 1 calculates the total of the list indices. Block 2 calculates the sum of the elements of the list.

59. **B**—Code inside the loop will never run because 10 > 5 before the loop runs the first time.

60. **D**—Each time the value in the list is not "banana," the word "banana" is appended to the end of the list.

61. **B**—Apples is in the 4th position in the list. snacks[4] = "apples".

62. **A**—The value at snacks[j] is replaced by number [j+4] which is 5, then 6, then 7, then 8 as j iterates through the values 1–4.

63. **B**—The plus + sign when used with text fields concatenates or glues them together.

64. **A**—None of the other options will produce better code or even code that works.

65. **B**—Programs developed for personal use do not have to have the same level of testing as apps that will handle sensitive transactions such as monetary ones or code that will be widely distributed.

66. **A**—This option is correct. The arrow is in the correct square and facing in the correct direction.

67. **B, D**—Cloud-based storage can be accessed from any location with an Internet connection, and is a good solution for storage when local storage options are limited. Sensitive data should not be stored in the cloud.

68. **C, D**—If aggregation is not done accurately, other data could be used in combination with the trial data and available public information to identify participants.

69. **C, D**—A team with diverse skills and backgrounds can provide different viewpoints that can result in a better product in a collaborative environment.

70. **A, D**—TCP makes the packets and puts them back together while IP sends them across the Internet.

71. **B, C**—Public key encryption creates such long keys that brute force techniques are ineffective. The keys are asymmetric meaning different keys are used to encrypt and decrypt the data.

72. **A, B**—A bit can only hold two possible values, 0 and 1. Therefore, any data it holds can only be represented by these two values. Any number

MOD 2 will produce 0 or 1 and Boolean values are either true or false.

73. **A, D**—Sending transaction data off-site can present a security concern if the data is not encrypted. Public key encryption is unbreakable at this point in time, so privacy issues would not be a concern. Companies should test their disaster recovery plan by periodically bringing data back on-site to run on existing equipment. Compression issues could also occur as the data may be too large to send without it.

74. **A, B**—Both asynchronous and synchronous communication processes use the "cloud" or servers located remotely to enable communication.

# AP Computer Science Principles: Practice Exam 2

## Multiple-Choice Questions
### ANSWER SHEET

| | | |
|---|---|---|
| 1 (A) (B) (C) (D) | 26 (A) (B) (C) (D) | 51 (A) (B) (C) (D) |
| 2 (A) (B) (C) (D) | 27 (A) (B) (C) (D) | 52 (A) (B) (C) (D) |
| 3 (A) (B) (C) (D) | 28 (A) (B) (C) (D) | 53 (A) (B) (C) (D) |
| 4 (A) (B) (C) (D) | 29 (A) (B) (C) (D) | 54 (A) (B) (C) (D) |
| 5 (A) (B) (C) (D) | 30 (A) (B) (C) (D) | 55 (A) (B) (C) (D) |
| 6 (A) (B) (C) (D) | 31 (A) (B) (C) (D) | 56 (A) (B) (C) (D) |
| 7 (A) (B) (C) (D) | 32 (A) (B) (C) (D) | 57 (A) (B) (C) (D) |
| 8 (A) (B) (C) (D) | 33 (A) (B) (C) (D) | 58 (A) (B) (C) (D) |
| 9 (A) (B) (C) (D) | 34 (A) (B) (C) (D) | 59 (A) (B) (C) (D) |
| 10 (A) (B) (C) (D) | 35 (A) (B) (C) (D) | 60 (A) (B) (C) (D) |
| 11 (A) (B) (C) (D) | 36 (A) (B) (C) (D) | 61 (A) (B) (C) (D) |
| 12 (A) (B) (C) (D) | 37 (A) (B) (C) (D) | 62 (A) (B) (C) (D) |
| 13 (A) (B) (C) (D) | 38 (A) (B) (C) (D) | 63 (A) (B) (C) (D) |
| 14 (A) (B) (C) (D) | 39 (A) (B) (C) (D) | 64 (A) (B) (C) (D) |
| 15 (A) (B) (C) (D) | 40 (A) (B) (C) (D) | 65 (A) (B) (C) (D) |
| 16 (A) (B) (C) (D) | 41 (A) (B) (C) (D) | 66 (A) (B) (C) (D) |
| 17 (A) (B) (C) (D) | 42 (A) (B) (C) (D) | 67 (A) (B) (C) (D) |
| 18 (A) (B) (C) (D) | 43 (A) (B) (C) (D) | 68 (A) (B) (C) (D) |
| 19 (A) (B) (C) (D) | 44 (A) (B) (C) (D) | 69 (A) (B) (C) (D) |
| 20 (A) (B) (C) (D) | 45 (A) (B) (C) (D) | 70 (A) (B) (C) (D) |
| 21 (A) (B) (C) (D) | 46 (A) (B) (C) (D) | 71 (A) (B) (C) (D) |
| 22 (A) (B) (C) (D) | 47 (A) (B) (C) (D) | 72 (A) (B) (C) (D) |
| 23 (A) (B) (C) (D) | 48 (A) (B) (C) (D) | 73 (A) (B) (C) (D) |
| 24 (A) (B) (C) (D) | 49 (A) (B) (C) (D) | 74 (A) (B) (C) (D) |
| 25 (A) (B) (C) (D) | 50 (A) (B) (C) (D) | |

# AP Computer Science Principles: Practice Exam 2

## Multiple-Choice Questions

Time: 2 hours
Number of questions: 74
The multiple-choice questions represent 60% of your total score.

Directions: Choose the one best answer for each question. Some questions at the end of the test have more than one correct answer; for these, you will be instructed to choose two answer choices.
Tear out the answer sheet on the previous page and grid in your answers using a pencil.
Consider how much time you have left before spending too much time on any one problem.

---

**AP Computer Science Principles Exam Reference Sheet**

On the AP Computer Science Principles Exam, you will be given a reference sheet to use while you're taking the multiple-choice test. A copy of this seven-page reference sheet is included in the Appendix of this book (reprinted by permission from the College Board).

To make taking this practice test like taking the actual exam, you should tear out the reference sheet so you can easily refer to it while taking the test.

If you tore out the pages earlier and have lost them, the reference sheet is also available near the end of the PDF publication, "Assessment Overview and Performance Task Directions for Students" on the College Board website. Here is the URL:

https://apcentral.collegeboard.org/pdf/ap-csp-student-task-directions.
    pdf?course=ap-computer-science-principles

1. When running a program that counts the number of records in a large data set, you receive an error on your computer screen, in hexadecimal format: F1.
Convert the error message from hexadecimal to decimal to be able to look it up.

    (A) 239 – Invalid operation. Corrupt data caused the error.
    (B) 240 – Decimal numbers are stored imprecisely in computers. A rounding error occurred.
    (C) 241 – Overflow error. The object exceeded its maximum size. The data set is too large to run on your computer.
    (D) 404 – Error message not found.

2. You read in the news about an employee who took advantage of decimal numbers used with currency exchanges to steal money. What is the most likely way the employee accomplished this?

    (A) The employee redirected the overflow amount when it occurred and deposited it in his account.
    (B) The employee took advantage of rounding and deposited the fractional amounts.
    (C) The amount is represented in binary and when the right-most bit was a 1, he replaced it with a 0 and deposited the difference.
    (D) Amount is represented in hexadecimal and in the conversion to decimal, he replaced an F with an E and deposited the difference.

3. You want to buy a ticket for a concert, but need to save enough money first. You know there are 5,000 seats in the venue, but they accidentally display the number of seats left in hexadecimal. If the number showing is $E8_{16}$, what is the decimal equivalent?

    (A) 232
    (B) 148
    (C) 3864
    (D) 562

4. You want to match the color for your favorite college team. The color you want to use is listed in decimal as (75, 156, 211). Which color is it, given options with hexadecimal equivalents for (Red, Green, Blue)?

    (A) #B49C133
    (B) #411C9134
    (C) #4B9CD3
    (D) #B4C93D

5. A group of students is collaborating to design an app to let students reserve a study room in the library. They are trying to decide how to check a room's availability. Which suggestion below is best and why?

    (A) Using real-time processing to ensure the app has current information
    (B) Creating a loop to prevent the student from over-writing another room reservation
    (C) Creating a procedure named "checkroom" because it can be called for each room and time slot
    (D) Directing students to the phone number to call the library to confirm their reservation

6. What order should the following procedures be used in creating the app from Question 5?

    - checkAvail()—checks the availability of the time requested since multiple people can use the app at the same time
    - recordResv()—records the room reservation
    - requestTime()—asks for a reservation time for the study room
    - timesAvail()—displays the times the room is available
    - updateTimes()—updates the times available to be displayed

    (A) requestTime(), recordResv(), timesAvail(), checkAvail(), updateTimes()
    (B) requestTime(), timesAvail(), recordResv(), updateTimes()
    (C) timesAvail(), requestTime(), checkAvail(), recordResv(), updateTimes()
    (D) requestTime(), recordResv(), updateTimes()

GO ON TO THE NEXT PAGE

**Questions 7 and 8 are based on the code below.**

Assume the variables and list already have values.

```
IF (topSongs[i] = song AND song_Times_Played = 100)
    REMOVE (topSongs, i)
ELSE
    play (song)
    song_Times_Played ← song_Times_Played + 1
```

7. What is the code doing?

(A) Playing a song from the topSongs list
(B) If a song is in topSongs, playing it, then removing it
(C) Removing song from topSongs if it has been played 100 times, otherwise playing the song and increasing the number of times played
(D) This code will not run as written.

8. In the above code, after a song has been deleted from the list once, it keeps being removed after the user adds it back to the list. What is the best way to fix this error?

(A) Change the program to allow songs to be played 1,000 times before being deleted.
(B) Send the user a message to confirm they want to delete the song stating it can never be added back to the list.
(C) Write a new procedure to add a song back to the list if it had been on the list previously.
(D) Set song_Times_Played back to 0 after removing a song.

9. An airplane simulation to train new pilots on typical take-offs and landings is designed specifically for cargo planes. Which variable does NOT need to be included?

(A) Weight of aircraft
(B) Number of crew for the airplane
(C) Where the cargo is located in the cargo hold
(D) Number of monthly bird strikes for this type of aircraft

10. If a program is expecting a data field to contain a string, using the section of the ASCII table below, how will the code interpret the binary number 01101010 for that data field?

| Decimal | Hexadecimal | Binary | Octal | Char |
|---|---|---|---|---|
| 97 | 61 | 01100001 | 141 | a |
| 98 | 62 | 01100010 | 142 | b |
| 99 | 63 | 01100011 | 143 | c |
| 100 | 64 | 01100100 | 144 | d |
| 101 | 65 | 01100101 | 145 | e |
| 102 | 66 | 01100110 | 146 | f |
| 103 | 67 | 01100111 | 147 | g |
| 104 | 68 | 01101000 | 150 | h |
| 105 | 69 | 01101001 | 151 | i |
| 106 | 6A | 01101010 | 152 | j |
| 107 | 6B | 01101011 | 153 | k |
| 108 | 6C | 01101100 | 154 | l |
| 109 | 6D | 01101101 | 155 | m |
| 110 | 6E | 01101110 | 156 | n |
| 111 | 6F | 01101111 | 157 | o |
| 112 | 70 | 01110000 | 160 | p |
| 113 | 71 | 01110001 | 161 | q |
| 114 | 72 | 01110010 | 162 | r |
| 115 | 73 | 01110011 | 163 | s |
| 116 | 74 | 01110100 | 164 | t |
| 117 | 75 | 01110101 | 165 | u |
| 118 | 76 | 01110110 | 166 | v |
| 119 | 77 | 01110111 | 167 | w |
| 120 | 78 | 01111000 | 170 | x |
| 121 | 79 | 01111001 | 171 | y |
| 122 | 7A | 01111010 | 172 | z |

(A) 106
(B) 6A
(C) 152
(D) j

GO ON TO THE NEXT PAGE

**11.** Which of the following will evaluate to false?

```
  i. false AND (true OR NOT(false))
 ii. true AND (NOT(true AND false))
iii. NOT (false OR (true OR false))
```

(A) i and ii
(B) ii and iii
(C) i and iii
(D) i, ii, and iii

**12.** Which of the following will evaluate to true?

```
  i. (true OR false) AND
     NOT(true OR NOT(false))
 ii. NOT (true AND
     (NOT(true OR false)))
iii. (NOT(true) OR (true AND false))
```

(A) i
(B) ii
(C) i and iii
(D) ii and iii

**13.** A group that is watching sea turtle nests records data about their nests. Which of the following is metadata?

(A) Daily temperature of the nest
(B) Date the eggs were laid
(C) Nest tag
(D) Number of data fields tracked

**14.** The video the nest watchers took of the baby sea turtles making their way to the water is too large to send. How can the volunteers compress the video to get it to the scientists in full resolution?

(A) Lossless compression will allow the scientists to see the video in full resolution.
(B) Lossy compression will make the file small enough to send.
(C) They should be combined for the best compression.
(D) Any compression technique will be sufficient.

**15.** When listening to an online music service, you see some ads local to your location. How does the music site determine what ads to show you?

(A) It shows ads based on the bands you listen to and where the band members grew up.
(B) It shows ads based on the location of the bands' current tour.

(C) It uses the location feature on the device playing the music.
(D) It plays a random selection of ads and you just notice the local ones more.

**16.** Which of the following techniques would be best to use to further analyze patterns that emerged during data mining?

i. Classifying data to categorize it into distinct groups.
ii. Cleaning data to determine which data to include in the processing.
iii. Clustering data to separate data with similarities into subclasses.
iv. Filtering to set conditions so only records meeting the criteria are included.

(A) i, ii, iii
(B) i, iii, iv
(C) i, ii, iv
(D) i, ii, iii, iv

**17.** A new discovery has been made from analyzing data. Which of the following methods will most effectively share the discovery?

(A) Create a video explaining the highlights and wait for it to go viral.
(B) Use diagrams and images and publish the discovery on a professional website for peer review.
(C) Post it on the Web but with a password to ensure only those in the field of study can view it.
(D) Publish the findings in a local newspaper.

**18.** New data is available to add to a company's existing data. The IT director wants to store the new data on the cloud. What is a concern that needs to be addressed before implementing the plan?

(A) The security of the data being transmitted back and forth
(B) The latency delay in requesting and receiving access to the data
(C) The redundancy of the Internet increasing the cost
(D) The cost the ISP will charge to access the cloud

GO ON TO THE NEXT PAGE

19. A good business practice is to send a copy of data off-site in the event of a catastrophic event such as a fire at the organization's primary location. How can organizations keep their data secure while transmitting and storing in an off-site location?

(A) They should encrypt their data using public key encryption.
(B) They should use a Caesar cipher to protect their data.
(C) They should only send non-sensitive data off-site.
(D) They should make physical copies of their data and ship it to the off-site location weekly.

20. In putting together a team, the project manager wants to have members with different backgrounds, even if they are in non-related fields. What is the best reason for this idea?

(A) Different experiences will help develop leaders on the team.
(B) There will be support for the project from all areas that have team members involved.
(C) The team members will ensure the project excels in their area of expertise.
(D) Different perspectives will help develop a better product.

21. What should an organization with fluctuating data storage needs consider?

(A) Using server farms for scalable solutions as data needs change
(B) Keeping all processing on-site
(C) Downsizing to maintain a more consistent data flow
(D) Duplicating business processing to ensure correctness

22. Which of the following will help organizations gain insights about their business?

(A) Collecting and analyzing big data to identify patterns and trends they can use to their advantage
(B) Separating big data into smaller data sets and analyzing those for faster results

(C) Developing decryption data techniques to be able to drill down and analyze data the government posts online
(D) Creating copies of company data to let each division do their own analysis without impacting others

23. How does the end-to-end architecture of the Internet work?

(A) It's designed like a circle; so ironically, there are no "ends".
(B) Packets are created at the sender's end and reassembled at the receiver's end.
(C) It uses HTML to share documents among users when requested through their web browsers.
(D) It creates redundancy, so when part of the Internet is down, information can keep flowing.

24. How do Internet packets travel to their destination?

(A) Router to router based on the Travelling Salesman algorithm
(B) Along the same path to stay in order
(C) Timed to arrive at the destination in their correct order
(D) Along a variety of different paths

25. What is an Internet Protocol (IP) and why are protocols used?

(A) Protocols are a set of rules used to ensure packets can be transmitted across different equipment used with the Internet.
(B) Protocols are procedures used to police the Internet.
(C) Protocols classify the data into clusters used for Internet traffic analysis.
(D) Protocols measure the latency on the Internet to determine the fastest path to send the data.

26. Which web address is the third-level domain?

http://anytime.anyway.anyplace.edu/apcsp

(A) anyway.anyplace.edu
(B) anytime.anyway.anyplace.edu
(C) anyplace.edu/apcsp
(D) edu

GO ON TO THE NEXT PAGE

27. What is bandwidth?

    (A) The amount of data that can be transmitted in a specified amount of time
    (B) The speed that data can be downloaded
    (C) The size of the cable that connects homes and businesses to the Internet
    (D) The type of wireless access point in use at a location

28. How can consumers ensure that a website is not a phishing scam before making an Internet purchase?

    (A) Go to the website directly rather than clicking a link from an email.
    (B) Call the company directly to be safe.
    (C) Use antivirus software and keep it up to date.
    (D) Use a firewall to block malware.

29. What is a cybersecurity attack that floods a website with too many requests causing it to slow down or crash?

    (A) A Man-in-the-Middle (MITM) attack because the website is surrounded by devices attacking it
    (B) A firewall breach because the attackers only need one "brick in the wall" to crack to gain entry
    (C) A Distributed Denial-of-Service (DDoS) attack because the website requests come from multiple locations
    (D) A net-phishing attack, which casts a wide "net of requests" over the website

30. What are brute-force attacks?

    (A) Attacks that use frequency analysis to break passwords
    (B) Attacks that check each possible solution to break encrypted data
    (C) Attacks against DNS servers to enable DDoS attacks
    (D) Attacks on firewalls to gain access to a company's sensitive data

31. Where should a company that is expanding to a new region place their data and why?

    (A) It should duplicate the data at both locations to provide backup and redundancy.
    (B) It should keep the data at headquarters and use dedicated lines to keep the data secure.
    (C) Half the data should be at each location to reduce the demand on the servers and reduce latency.
    (D) It should place their data in the cloud so everyone can reach it at any time.

32. Why is the Internet designed to be fault tolerant?

    (A) People often have typos in their web requests and fault tolerance prevents the system from crashing when these occur.
    (B) So the Internet can keep running even when it has malware.
    (C) So it can keep running when sections of it are not working.
    (D) So as companies move from IPv4 to IPv6, conflicts can be resolved.

33. Advances in sensor technology have had many benefits. Which of the following is **NOT** an advance in assistive technology to help people live more independently?

    (A) Sensors can be connected to contact family members or emergency services.
    (B) Sensors can help people call for help if they fall.
    (C) Sensors can turn off appliances.
    (D) Sensors can guide wheelchairs to automatically load and unload people into their vehicles.

34. While crowdsourcing is often used to fund projects, what is another use in practice today?

    (A) Diagnosing medical conditions by asking if others have similar symptoms
    (B) Asking those who register with a company to evaluate new products
    (C) Lowering costs by using the crowd's computers
    (D) Matching people needing work with job openings

GO ON TO THE NEXT PAGE

**35.** If data mining identifies new patterns, what should a company do with the information?

(A) Further analyze the data pattern identified to make strategic decisions.

(B) Change the prices on their products to match the findings for increased sales.

(C) Get their products to market faster to increase their profit.

(D) Use it to place targeted ads with people who are repeat customers.

**36.** What is the purpose of the DMCA?

(A) To provide protection for intellectual property in digital format that has copyright status

(B) To enable music and movie downloads and streaming for wider sharing of people's creative works

(C) To give acknowledgment to the creator of a digital work when it is used by others

(D) To provide the software to share digital files legally

**37.** Which code segment will correctly add a name to a team roster?

Assume all variables and lists are appropriately initialized.

**Block 1**

```
REPEAT UNTIL x ≤ 0
{
    APPEND (roster, name)
    x ← x + 1
}
```

Block 2

```
FOR EACH name IN roster
{
    APPEND (roster, name)
    DISPLAY(name)
}
```

(A) Block 1

(B) Block 2

(C) Both Block 1 and Block 2

(D) Neither Block 1 nor Block 2

**38.** Which algorithm will determine if a number is even?

(A)
```
num ← INPUT( )
IF (num MOD 2 = 0)
{
        DISPLAY (num, " is even")
}
```

(B)
```
/* assume list is initialized with
   integers */
FOR Each num IN list
{
  IF (num / 2 = 0)
  {
        DISPLAY (num, " is even")
  }
}
```

(C)
```
num ← INPUT( )
IF ((num / 2) * num = num)
{
        DISPLAY (num, " is even")
}
```

(D)
```
num ← INPUT( )
IF (NOT (num MOD 2 = 0))
{
        DISPLAY(num, " is even")
}
```

**39.** Why is a binary search the most effective way to search a sorted data set?

(A) The item searched for bubbles to the beginning of the data set after one pass.

(B) It uses machine learning with each pass of the data to learn where the data is located in the file to speed up the search process.

(C) It eliminates half the data set with each iteration of the search.

(D) It merges sections of data to only have to search one section with each iteration.

**40.** Which of these is NOT a Boolean expression?

(A) `IF (eyes = brown AND height > 60)`
(B) `REPEAT UNTIL (song = favSong)`
(C) `IF (NOT(pet = cat))`
(D) `x ← (x + 42)`

GO ON TO THE NEXT PAGE

41. If a programmer tested the following code with the values indicated, would the program correctly calculate the average of the test scores?

    Assume all variables and lists have been appropriately initialized.

```
FOR EACH score IN testScores
{
    IF score > 0
    {
            total ← total + score
    }
    count ← count + 1
}
DISPLAY ("The average score on the
test was: ", total / count)
```

```
Test1 [100, 90, 80, 80, 85, 50, 0, 85,
 90]
Test2 [192, 85, 74, 100, 96, 88]
```

    (A) Yes, the code works as it should for both test cases.
    (B) No, the code does not average the test scores correctly for either test.
    (C) No, the code only works for the Test1 scores.
    (D) No, the code only works for the Test2 scores.

42. A high school has two rows of lockers. Even numbered lockers are on the top row and odd numbered lockers are on the bottom. Do the following two algorithms correctly calculate which lockers should be counted as even numbered ones for the top row and which should be counted as odd numbered lockers for the bottom row?

**Block 1**

```
IF (count MOD 2 = 1)
{
   topLocker ← topLocker + 1
}
```

**Block 2**

```
IF (NOT (count MOD 2 = 1))
{
   bottomLocker ← bottomLocker + 1
}
```

    (A) Block 1 works correctly.
    (B) Block 2 works correctly.
    (C) Both blocks work correctly.
    (D) Neither block works correctly.

43. If a large file has multiple duplicates in it that should be removed prior to using it for analysis, in what order should the following procedures be called?

```
  i. ProcessFile( )
 ii. RemoveDuplicates( )
iii. SortFile( )
```

    (A) i, ii, iii
    (B) i, iii, ii
    (C) iii, ii, i
    (D) ii, iii, i

44. When should a heuristic algorithm be used?

    (A) When a problem is intractable but a "close enough" solution is acceptable
    (B) When the data is not sorted and cannot be placed in the order needed
    (C) When a problem is undecidable because not enough information is known
    (D) When searching is needed but efficiency is a requirement

45. How many times do FOR EACH loops run with lists?

    (A) Once
    (B) Until the index for the list is 0
    (C) For the LENGTH of the list
    (D) Until the user types STOP

46. Which code below can replace the missing code to select data that is less than the targetValue and even? Assume all variables have been properly initialized.

```
IF /* missing code */
{
   DISPLAY ("Found it!")
}
```

    (A) (num MOD 2 = 0) OR (targetValue < num)
    (B) (targetValue > num) AND (targetValue MOD 2 = 0)
    (C) (num MOD 2 = 0) AND (targetValue > num)
    (D) (targetValue > num) OR (NOT(num MOD 2 > 0))

GO ON TO THE NEXT PAGE

47. Which type(s) of statement is needed to find all records in a list that are positive?

    (A) Sequential and iterative
    (B) Selection and sequential
    (C) Selection
    (D) Iterative and selection

48. Grace and Ada write algorithms and test them with increasingly large data sets. Algorithm 1 is still running while algorithm 2 completed before midnight. What can you determine about the algorithms?

    (A) One is intractable and two is tractable.
    (B) One is tractable and two is intractable.
    (C) One is unsolvable and two is decidable.
    (D) One is decidable and two is unsolvable.

49. Each of the following can make an algorithm more readable except:

    (A) Well-named variables and procedures
    (B) Consistent formatting within the code
    (C) Procedures that have one purpose
    (D) Minimizing the use of loops so the program flow will be clearer

50. For a block of code under an ELSE statement to run, the selection criteria result must be which of the following?

    (A) Repetitive
    (B) Compound
    (C) True
    (D) False

51. Which set of pseudocode will correctly cause an alarm clock to chime at the correct time?

    (A) Compare alarm time to current time
        If the times are not equal, check am/pm indicator
        If am/pm is equal, turn on alarm

    (B) Compare alarm time to current time
        If the times are equal, check am/pm indicator
        If am/pm is equal, turn on alarm

    (C) Compare alarm am/pm indicator to time am/pm
        If not equal, compare alarm time to current time
        If the times are equal, turn on alarm

    (D) Compare alarm am/pm indicator to time am/pm
        If not equal, compare alarm time to current time
        If the times are not equal, turn on alarm

52. Which diagram matches the code below?

```
MOVE_FORWARD(2)
ROTATE_LEFT(3)
MOVE_FORWARD(3)
ROTATE_RIGHT(1)
MOVE_FORWARD(1)
ROTATE_LEFT(3)
MOVE_FORWARD(1)
ROTATE_RIGHT(3)
```

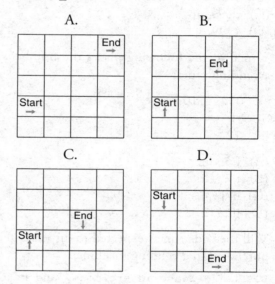

53. You need to swap the first and last values in a list. Which option produces the correct process?

    (A) list[1] ← list[LENGTH]
        list[LENGTH] ← list[1]

    (B) tempValue ← list[LENGTH]
        list[1] ← tempValue
        list[LENGTH] ← list[1]

    (C) tempValue ← list[LENGTH]
        list[LENGTH] ← list[1]
        list[1] ← tempValue

    (D) tempValue ← list[LENGTH]
        list[1] ← tempValue
        list[LENGTH] ← list[tempValue]

GO ON TO THE NEXT PAGE

**54.** What is the value of carChk after the code below runs?

```
PROCEDURE carMaint (miles)
{
   checkUp ← false
   IF (miles ≥ 4999)
   {
      checkUp ← true
   }
   RETURN (checkUp)
}

carChk ← carMaint(4999)
```

(A) False
(B) True
(C) check up
(D) 4999

**55.** Which of the following places the numbers in ascending order?

  i. 01011110
  ii. 5F
  iii. 72

(A) i, ii, iii.
(B) i, iii, ii.
(C) ii, iii, i.
(D) iii, i, ii.

**56.** Will the code run as expected to dispense items purchased in a vending machine?

```
DISPLAY("Please insert money and make
  a selection")
amtPaid ← INPUT( )

REPEAT UNTIL (amtPaid ≥ cost)
{
    DISPLAY("Please enter $ ", cost -
      amtPaid, "to make your purchase")
    amtPaid ← amtPaid + INPUT( )
}

IF (amtPaid > cost)
{
    DISPLAY ("Your change is
      $", (cost - amtPaid))
    Dispense(item)
    Dispense(change)
}
ELSE
{
    Dispense(item)
}
DISPLAY("Enjoy your selection!")
```

(A) Yes, the code works as expected.
(B) The REPEAT UNTIL loop is an infinite loop.
(C) The calculation of the amount of change to return is incorrect.
(D) The > sign should be < in the IF statement.

**57.** What is displayed after the following code runs?

```
rate ← 10
hours ← 40
totalPay ← 0
overtimePay ← 0
```

```
IF ( hours > 40 )

    DISPLAY("You earned overtime pay.")

ELSE

    DISPLAY("Regular Pay = $", hours * rate)
```

(A) You earned overtime pay.
(B) Regular Pay = $40 * 10
(C) 400
(D) Regular Pay = $400

**58.** How many times does the following loop run?

```
numSold ← true
price ← x

REPEAT numSold TIMES
{
     sales ← numSold * price
     numSold ← numSold -1
}
```

(A) The REPEAT loop will run 5 times.
(B) The REPEAT loop executes once and exits the loop after numSold's value changes.
(C) The REPEAT loop never ends creating an infinite loop because numSold's value keeps changing.
(D) The program has an error and will not run.

GO ON TO THE NEXT PAGE

**Questions 59–61 refer to the following code.**

```
count ← 1
pets ← ["dog", "dogfood", "cat",
 "catfood", "fish"]
FOR EACH animal IN pets
{
    IF (animal = "fish")
    {
        DISPLAY animal
        INSERT(pets, count, "fishfood")
    }
    count ← count + 1
}
```

**59.** What will the code display?

(A) dog, dogfood, cat, catfood, fish
(B) dog, dogfood, cat, catfood, fish, fishfood
(C) fish, fishfood
(D) fish

**60.** What is the length of the list "pets" after the code runs?

(A) 4
(B) 5
(C) 6
(D) 7

**61.** What is value of pets[3] after the following code is run?

```
j ← 1
INSERT (pets, 1, "horse")
INSERT (pets, 2, "carrots")
REMOVE (pets, 3)
```

(A) It is an empty field.
(B) dog
(C) dogfood
(D) cat

**62.** While cookies have advantages such as convenience and personalization, what is a concern with the use of cookies?

(A) Targeted advertising
(B) Cookies taking up storage on your device
(C) Privacy of personal data
(D) Increased latency on the browser requests

**63.** What should project teams do to produce a better software product?

(A) Break down the problem into manageable units.
(B) Code while requirements are being finalized.
(C) Reduce the testing step to the more complicated conditions only.
(D) Not allow any changes from the user.

**64.** A soccer league tracks certain stats by team as seen in the table below. Which of the following CANNOT be determined by the data?

(A) If a team wins more often when the number of red cards is less than 1 per game
(B) If a team wins more when they were the home team
(C) If days where the temperature was 80°F were also rainy
(D) Team winning percentage

| Team # | Wins | Losses | Average number of red cards per game | Game day temperature higher than 80°F | Rain day before a game | Home games won |
|--------|------|--------|------|------|------|------|
| 55 | 22 | 12 | 0 | 17 | 10 | 19 |
| 42 | 11 | 23 | 1.5 | 13 | 15 | 4 |
| 37 | 19 | 15 | 0.5 | 14 | 17 | 12 |

GO ON TO THE NEXT PAGE

**65.** What is this block of code doing?

```
price ← p
numItems ← num
taxRate ← foodTax
amtPaid ← 20.00
inv ← currInv
amtOwe ← (price * numItems) * taxRate
IF (amtPaid ≥ amtOwe)
{
        change ← amtPaid - amtOwe
        inv ← inv - 1
}
ELSE
{
        DISPLAY("Please pay an
         additional $", amtOwe - amtPaid)
}
```

   i. Calculates the tax for an item.

  ii. Calculates current inventory numbers.

 iii. Calculates the change owed the customer or if the customer needs to pay more for their purchase.

(A) i and ii

(B) i and iii

(C) ii and iii

(D) i, ii, and iii

**66.** Which set of code will move the robot from start to stop? The robot may not use gray blocks.

| | | | | Start ↓ |
|---|---|---|---|---|
| | | | | |
| | | | | |
| | | | | |
| | Stop ↑ | | | |

(A)
```
MOVE_FORWARD(2)
ROTATE_RIGHT(1)
MOVE_FORWARD(4)
ROTATE_LEFT(1)
MOVE_FORWARD(2)
ROTATE_RIGHT(1)
MOVE_FORWARD(1)
ROTATE_LEFT(1)
```

(B)
```
MOVE_FORWARD(3)
ROTATE_LEFT(3)
MOVE_FORWARD(2)
ROTATE_LEFT(1)
MOVE_FORWARD(1)
ROTATE_LEFT(3)
MOVE_FORWARD(1)
ROTATE_LEFT(3)
```

(C)
```
MOVE_FORWARD(3)
ROTATE_RIGHT(3)
MOVE_FORWARD(2)
ROTATE_RIGHT(1)
MOVE_FORWARD(1)
ROTATE_RIGHT(3)
MOVE_FORWARD(1)
ROTATE_RIGHT(3)
```

(D)
```
MOVE_FORWARD(1)
MOVE_FORWARD(1)
ROTATE_RIGHT(1)
MOVE_FORWARD(1)
MOVE_FORWARD(1)
MOVE_FORWARD(1)
ROTATE_LEFT(1)
MOVE_FORWARD(1)
MOVE_FORWARD(1)
```

**67.** Which of the algorithms below will produce the same result? Select two answers.

(A) Processing a list from the beginning to the end and counting the number of elements that begin with the letter "a"

(B) Processing a list from the end to the beginning and counting the number of elements that begin with the letter "a"

(C) Processing the list with a merge search to group the elements that begin with "a" and then counting them

(D) Processing the list with a procedure to see if the element begins with the letter "a" and keeping count with a local variable

**68.** An alarm company records the number of times each door is opened and closed. The alarm cannot be set if a door is still open. How can the alarm company code this option in their software? Select two answers.

(A) If the door count multiplied by 2 gives an odd number, then the door is open.

(B) If door MOD 2 = 1, then the door is open.

(C) If the number of times a door is opened does not equal the number of times it is closed, then the door is open.

(D) If the quotient of dividing the door count by two is an even number, then the door is open.

GO ON TO THE NEXT PAGE

69. A simulation for a new app to allow students to place a lunch order by 11:00 a.m. to speed up the lunch line is being tested. What information will the simulation provide? Select two answers.

    (A) If a new line at the pick-up station will cause a slowdow
    (B) If students will use the app often enough to make it worth the cost of developing
    (C) If the app will decrease the cost of wasted food
    (D) If the app can speed up the lunch line

70. If two people need to collaborate on a document but are in two different locations, what is the best solution? Select two answers.

    (A) One person needs to travel to the other person's location.
    (B) Assign a different person to work on the document that is located in the same place as one of the others.
    (C) Use a cloud-based service for the document so both can edit it.
    (D) Hold video conferences for them to speak face to face to discuss the document.

71. Why are "citizen scientists" being used on projects? Select two answers.

    (A) They can record local data to be included in global databases.
    (B) They are paid minimum wage.
    (C) They can record data over a longer period of time.
    (D) To keep retired scientists involved in their area of expertise.

72. Which of the following are data aggregation techniques used to protect privacy? Select two answers.

    (A) Removing names from the data records
    (B) Changing all patient names to the same name
    (C) Adding a check digit to the zip code
    (D) Grouping the data based on zip codes

73. How has communication changed with cloud computing? Select two answers.

    (A) It has facilitated asynchronous communication with email and text messaging.
    (B) It has facilitated synchronous methods with video conferencing.
    (C) Small businesses fall further behind large companies as they cannot afford to take advantage of the cloud computing communication benefits.
    (D) Confidential communications are being sent via the postal service to ensure they remain secure.

74. Which of the following are benefits resulting from technological innovations in education? Select two answers.

    (A) Online courses are available if a school cannot teach a specific course.
    (B) Online textbooks are available during the school day.
    (C) Classes can participate in virtual field trips.
    (D) The digital divide is minimizing the gap of educational opportunities available to all.

**STOP. End of Exam**

# AP Computer Science Principles: Practice Exam 2

## Answers and Explanations

1. **C**—The number was larger than the computer could handle resulting in an overflow error.

2. **B**—The way floating point numbers are stored can cause rounding errors. The employee sent the fractional part of numbers to the separate account and it accumulated over time. For example, if the number was $1.988889, then $ 0.008889 could be sent to the extra account.

3. **A**—Take the hexadecimal number and convert each individual number to its binary equivalent using 4 bits.

   E → 14 → 1110          8 → 1000

   Then convert the binary number to decimal. Write the table for the powers of 2 on the side of your paper so you do not make an error. For every column there is a 1 in the binary number, add the corresponding value of $2^x$.

   | $2^7$ | $2^6$ | $2^5$ | $2^4$ | $2^3$ | $2^2$ | $2^1$ | $2^0$ |
   |-----|-----|-----|-----|-----|-----|-----|-----|
   | 128 | 64  | 32  | 16  | 8   | 4   | 2   | 1   |
   | 1   | 1   | 1   | 0   | 1   | 0   | 0   | 0   |

   $$128 + 64 + 32 + 8 = 232_{10}$$

4. **C**—You need to convert the number for each color from decimal to hexadecimal: 75 for Red, 156 for Green, 211 for Blue. First convert the decimal number to binary.

   $75_{10} = 0100\ 1011_2$   $156_{10} = 1001\ 1100_2$
   $211_{10} = 1101\ 0011_2$

   Then convert the binary to the hexadecimal equivalent using the 4 bits shortcut.

   Red: 4  11 → 4B    Green:  9 12 → 9C
   Blue: 13 3 → D3

   RGB (75, 156, 211) = #4B9CD3

5. **C**—A procedure that can be called to check availability is the best solution. It avoids duplication of code and does not force the student to pick a time.

6. **C**—The program should display available times so people can see if the time they want is available. They can then request a time. The app should check to ensure the time has not already been taken since multiple people can use the app at the same time. Then the reservation can be recorded and the list of available times updated.

7. **C**—If the song has already been played 100 times, it will be removed from the list topSongs. Otherwise, it will be played and the number of times played will increase by 1.

8. **D**—The number of times the song has been played is still set to 100, so even after the user adds it back to the list, then the next time it is played, both conditions in the IF statement will be true and it will be removed again. Resetting it back to 0 after it has been removed from the list is the best way to resolve the problem.

9. **D**—The number bird strikes are not needed to practice typical take-offs and landings.

10. **D**—A string is a text field so the binary numbers will represent letters. Find the binary number on the table and then the corresponding letter associated with it.

11. **C**—The first and third conditions evaluate to be false. The only time an OR condition is false is when both are false, and the NOT operator takes the opposite of the value so true would become false and false would become true.

12. **B**—Only the second condition evaluates to true. Both values must be true with an AND to be true, and one or both need to be true with an OR for it to be true.

13. **D**—Metadata is data about data, and the number of data fields volunteers track is about the data. The other fields are data about the sea turtle nests.

14. **A**—Only the lossless compression technique will allow the original uncompressed video to be restored for the scientists to review.

15. **C**—Services use the location tracker on your device. There would have been a pop-up asking for permission to use your location. If you clicked OK, then you will hear and see local ads.

16. **D**—All of the methods can be used with further analysis.

17. **B**—Publishing the results in an easy to view format on a vetted website is the best method.

18. **A**—Transmitting company data back and forth is a security concern and encryption of the data is important to keep company data about customers, employees, and trade secrets secure.

19. **A**—Sending transaction data off-site can present a security concern if the data is not encrypted. Public key encryption has not been broken and is the standard today.

20. **D**—A team with diverse skills and backgrounds can result in a better product in a collaborative environment.

21. **A**—Server farms can provide solutions that can grow as needs grow.

22. **A**—Smaller data sets may not have enough data to identify patterns or true trends.

23. **B**—The Internet has an end-to-end architecture because packets are created by breaking the information into smaller segments at one end (the sender's), and are reassembled at the other end (the receiver's).

24. **D**—Packets travel along many different paths to reach their final destination. They arrive out of order and are then reassembled at the destination.

25. **A**—Protocols are rules that are followed to ensure data can communicate across all equipment.

26. **A**—The top-level domain is the highest level in the Domain Name System and is at the far right of a website name. The second-level domain is to the left of the top-level domain and the third-level domain is to the left of the second-level domain.

27. **A**—Bandwidth measures the amount of data that can be transmitted in a specific amount of time. Therefore, knowing how much data needs to be downloaded on a regular basis is a key measurement.

28. **A**—Phishing scams can make a website look very realistic. To be sure you are at an authentic website, search to find the link yourself or type it into your browser rather than clicking on a link.

29. **C**—A Distributed Denial-of-Service (DDoS) attack is one that floods a website with requests in an attempt to cause it to crash.

30. **B**—Brute force techniques try every solution to try and break through the protection around encrypted data.

31. **D**—The data should be moved to the cloud so all employees can access it any time with an Internet connection.

32. **C**—Fault tolerance means the Internet will continue to function and re-route packets when parts of it are down.

33. **D**—This is not an available assistive technology.

34. **D**—Crowdsourcing is used in many ways and more are coming into use. Helping people find available jobs is one use.

35. **A**—Companies should take the findings from the data-mining results and make strategic decisions to determine when and how to take advantage of the new information. The other decisions can be made based on current sales and projections and do not need data-mining techniques.

36. **A**—To protect intellectual property, the Digital Millennium Copyright Act works to prevent illegal file sharing, illegal downloads, and licensing violations.

37. **D**—Both blocks of code have an error. The first is an infinite loop, and Block 2 will add the new name multiple times.

38. **A**—The MOD operator returns the remainder when two numbers are divided. If a number is divided by 2 and the remainder is zero, then it is an even number.

39. **C**—The binary search is most efficient as a divide-and-conquer algorithm because half the data can be removed with each iteration of the search. The item can be found or determined that it is not in the dataset in a minimal number of passes.

40. **D**—Booleans can only be true or false; D is the only option that does not evaluate to true or false.

41. **D**—The code only includes test scores that are greater than 0. Test1 scores have a 0 that will not be included in the average, but it should. The IF statement should be removed to correctly calculate test averages in all cases.

42. **D**—Neither algorithms will correctly track if a locker is an even number (top locker) or an odd number (bottom locker).

43. **C**—The file should be sorted and duplicates removed; then it is ready for processing.

44. **A**—A heuristic is finding the best approximate solution when the actual solution is intractable.

45. **C**—FOR EACH loops will run for each element in a list.

46. **C**—To test if a number is even, you can use MOD with 2 and a remainder of 0 means it is even. Use less than "<" to determine if a number is less than another. Use AND for both conditions to be true to select the number. Be sure to use the correct variable, "num", to test the conditions.

47. **D**—Iterative code will loop until every item in the list is checked and a selection statement is needed to determine if a number is positive.

48. **A**—Tractable algorithms run efficiently for large and small data sets while intractable algorithms cannot run efficiently for large datasets.

49. **D**—Readability is a feature of algorithms that are clear and easy to understand. Every feature except D helps others understand what its intended purpose is. Loops should be used to shorten the code which makes it more readable.

50. **D**—The selection criteria must be false for the code associated with an ELSE to run.

51. **B**—Option B compares the time first, and if equal, it then checks the am/pm indicator.

52. **C**—This diagram starts and ends in the correct block facing in the correct direction. Remember that rotating left three times is the same as a right turn and rotating right three times is the same as a left turn.

53. **C**—The temporary variable is assigned the value at the end of the list. Then the last element can be assigned the value in the first position. Finally, the first position in the list is assigned the value in the temporary variable.

54. **B**—checkUp is set to true if miles ≥ 4999. Since miles is 4999, checkUp will be true.

55. **D**—The binary number $= 93_{10}$, the hexadecimal number $= 94_{10}$, so the numbers in ascending order go from decimal (72), binary (94), hexadecimal (95).

56. **C**—The amount of change due calculates a negative number. The calculation should be amtPaid – cost rather than cost – amtPaid.

57. **D**—The ELSE condition will run because hours is not greater than 40. Therefore, the program will display answer D.

58. **D**—The criteria for the REPEAT loop is incorrect. It must be a constant or a variable holding an integer value, not a Boolean value.

59. **D**—The only time the animal is displayed is when it is a fish.

60. **C**—The length of the list, pets, is 6 as there are 6 elements in it.

61. **C**—The INSERT command moves current values over a position each time.
The REMOVE command shifts list values to the left.
After these commands, pets[3] = dogfood

62. **C**—Privacy of your personal data is the main concern with the use of cookies. Since cookies track your browsing activity, others can access the information stored in them.

63. **A**—None of the other options will produce better or even code that works.

64. **C**—The only information that cannot be determined from the table is if it rained on days that were 80 degrees F or warmer.

65. **C**—The block of code calculates the current inventory, change owed if any, and the additional amount to pay, if any. It does not calculate the tax rate. That is provided and used to calculate the total amount due.

66. **B**—The code starts and stops in the correct block facing the correct direction. Remember that rotate blocks do not move forward. They rotate the direction within the current block.

67. **A, B**—Processing a list from the beginning to the end or the end to the beginning with the same code in each to find and count the elements that start with an "a" will produce the same results. A merge search does not exist (but a merge sort does). The local variable that counts the words would not be available outside of the procedure.

68. **B, C**—If one variable counts the number of door openings and closings, then modular math, which gives the remainder after division, can determine if a number is even or odd. An odd number would mean a door is open. Option C uses two variables for the same door, one to count the number of times a door opened and the other records the number of times it closed. If these are not the same, then a door is open and the alarm cannot be set.

69. **A, D**—The simulation can show if the lunch line will speed up and if a new bottleneck will be created at the pick-up line. The simulation will not show how often the app will be used or if food will be wasted.

70. **C, D**—Cloud-based storage can be accessed from any locations with an Internet connection and is a good solution for storage when people are in different locations. Video conferences will help the collaboration effort.

71. **A, C**—With training, "citizen scientists" can provide a wealth of data over longer periods of time and they could be anywhere in the world creating more data from a variety of locations.

72. **A, B**—If aggregation is not done accurately, trial data and available public information could be used to identify participants. Removing or changing all names will help protect identities. Too much public data is available for the zip code masking or grouping to protect people's privacy.

73. **A, B**—Both asynchronous and synchronous communication are enabled by the "cloud" or servers located remotely.

74. **A, C**—Online courses are now offered in many schools as an option for students seeking a course not offered in their school. A virtual field trip is also a possibility when an actual field trip is not possible. These new options resulting from technological innovations in education benefit students by providing new opportunities.

# Appendix

AP Computer Science Principles Exam Reference Sheet

# AP COMPUTER SCIENCE PRINCIPLES EXAM REFERENCE SHEET

As AP Computer Science Principles does not designate any particular programming language, this reference sheet provides instructions and explanations to help students understand the format and meaning of the questions they will see on the exam. The reference sheet includes two programming formats: text based and block based.

Programming instructions use four data types: numbers, Booleans, strings, and lists. Instructions from any of the following categories may appear on the exam:

- Assignment, Display, and Input
- Arithmetic Operators and Numeric Procedures
- Relational and Boolean Operators
- Selection
- Iteration
- List Operations
- Procedures
- Robot

| Instruction | Explanation |
|---|---|
| **Assignment, Display, and Input** ||
| Text:<br>`a ← expression`<br><br>Block:<br>`a ⟵ expression` | Evaluates `expression` and assigns the result to the variable `a`. |
| Text:<br>`DISPLAY (expression)`<br><br>Block:<br>`DISPLAY expression` | Displays the value of `expression`, followed by a space. |
| Text:<br>`INPUT ()`<br><br>Block:<br>`INPUT` | Accepts a value from the user and returns it. |
| **Arithmetic Operators and Numeric Procedures** ||
| Text and Block:<br>`a + b`<br>`a - b`<br>`a * b`<br>`a / b` | The arithmetic operators +, −, *, and / are used to perform arithmetic on `a` and `b`.<br><br>For example, `3 / 2` evaluates to `1.5`. |
| Text and Block:<br>`a MOD b` | Evaluates to the remainder when `a` is divided by `b`. Assume that `a` and `b` are positive integers.<br><br>For example, `17 MOD 5` evaluates to `2`. |
| Text:<br>`RANDOM (a, b)`<br><br>Block:<br>`RANDOM a, b` | Evaluates to a random integer from `a` to `b`, including `a` and `b`.<br><br>For example, `RANDOM (1, 3)` could evaluate to `1`, `2`, or `3`. |
| **Relational and Boolean Operators** ||
| Text and Block:<br>`a = b`<br>`a ≠ b`<br>`a > b`<br>`a < b`<br>`a ≥ b`<br>`a ≤ b` | The relational operators =, ≠, >, <, ≥, and ≤ are used to test the relationship between two variables, expressions, or values.<br><br>For example, `a = b` evaluates to `true` if `a` and `b` are equal; otherwise, it evaluates to `false`. |

| Instruction | Explanation |
|---|---|
| **Relational and Boolean Operators (continued)** | |
| Text:<br>`NOT condition`<br><br>Block:<br>`NOT (condition)` | Evaluates to `true` if condition is `false`; otherwise evaluates to `false`. |
| Text:<br>`condition1 AND condition2`<br><br>Block:<br>`(condition1) AND (condition2)` | Evaluates to `true` if both `condition1` and `condition2` are `true`; otherwise, evaluates to `false`. |
| Text:<br>`condition1 OR condition2`<br><br>Block:<br>`(condition1) OR (condition2)` | Evaluates to `true` if `condition1` is `true` or if `condition2` is `true` or if both `condition1` and `condition2` are `true`; otherwise, evaluates to `false`. |
| **Selection** | |
| Text:<br>`IF (condition)`<br>`{`<br>`    <block of statements>`<br>`}`<br><br>Block:<br>`IF (condition)`<br>`  (block of statements)` | The code in `block of statements` is executed if the Boolean expression `condition` evaluates to `true`; no action is taken if `condition` evaluates to `false`. |

| Instruction | Explanation |
|---|---|
| **Selection (continued)** | |
| Text:<br>`IF (condition)`<br>`{`<br>`    <first block of statements>`<br>`}`<br>`ELSE`<br>`{`<br>`    <second block of statements>`<br>`}`<br><br>Block:<br>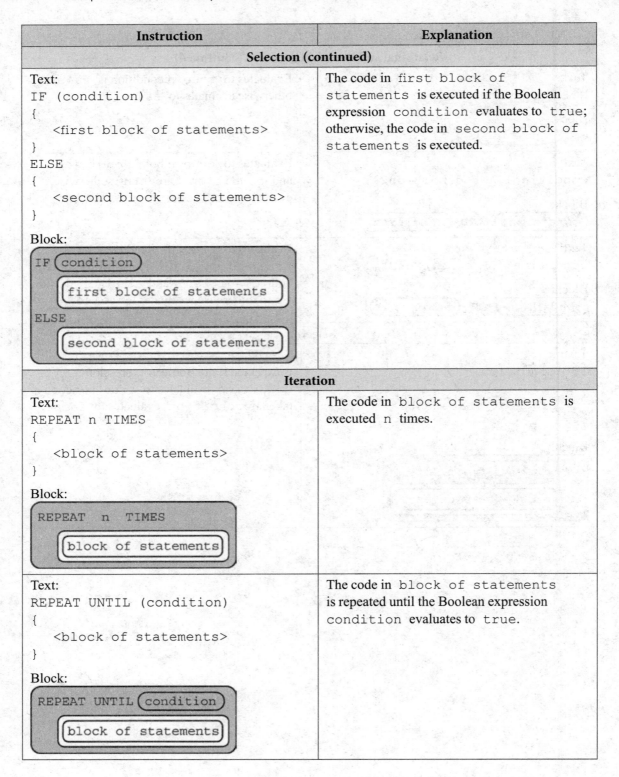 | The code in `first block of statements` is executed if the Boolean expression `condition` evaluates to `true`; otherwise, the code in `second block of statements` is executed. |
| **Iteration** | |
| Text:<br>`REPEAT n TIMES`<br>`{`<br>`    <block of statements>`<br>`}`<br><br>Block: | The code in `block of statements` is executed `n` times. |
| Text:<br>`REPEAT UNTIL (condition)`<br>`{`<br>`    <block of statements>`<br>`}`<br><br>Block: | The code in `block of statements` is repeated until the Boolean expression `condition` evaluates to `true`. |

| Instruction | Explanation |
|---|---|
| **List Operations** | |
| For all list operations, if a list index is less than 1 or greater than the length of the list, an error message is produced and the program terminates. | |
| Text:<br>`list[i]`<br><br>Block:<br>`list i` | Refers to the element of `list` at index `i`. The first element of `list` is at index `1`. |
| Text:<br>`list[i] ← list[j]`<br><br>Block:<br>`list i ← list j` | Assigns the value of `list[j]` to `list[i]`. |
| Text:<br>`list ← [value1, value2, value3]`<br><br>Block:<br>`list ← value1, value2, value3` | Assigns `value1`, `value2`, and `value3` to `list[1]`, `list[2]`, and `list[3]`, respectively. |
| Text:<br>`FOR EACH item IN list`<br>`{`<br>`    <block of statements>`<br>`}`<br><br>Block:<br>`FOR EACH item IN list`<br>`    block of statements` | The variable `item` is assigned the value of each element of `list` sequentially, in order from the first element to the last element. The code in `block of statements` is executed once for each assignment of `item`. |
| Text:<br>`INSERT (list, i, value)`<br><br>Block:<br>`INSERT list, i, value` | Any values in `list` at indices greater than or equal to `i` are shifted to the right. The length of list is increased by 1, and `value` is placed at index `i` in `list`. |
| Text:<br>`APPEND (list, value)`<br><br>Block:<br>`APPEND list, value` | The length of `list` is increased by 1, and `value` is placed at the end of `list`. |

| Instruction | Explanation |
|---|---|
| **List Operations (continued)** | |
| Text:<br>`REMOVE (list, i)`<br><br>Block:<br>`REMOVE list, i` | Removes the item at index `i` in `list` and shifts to the left any values at indices greater than `i`. The length of `list` is decreased by 1. |
| Text:<br>`LENGTH (list)`<br><br>Block:<br>`LENGTH list` | Evaluates to the number of elements in `list`. |
| **Procedures** | |
| Text:<br>`PROCEDURE name (parameter1,`<br>`            parameter2, ...)`<br>`{`<br>`    <instructions>`<br>`}`<br><br>Block:<br>`PROCEDURE name  parameter1,`<br>`                parameter2,...`<br>`    instructions` | A procedure, `name`, takes zero or more parameters. The procedure contains programming instructions. |
| Text:<br>`PROCEDURE name (parameter1,`<br>`            parameter2, ...)`<br>`{`<br>`    <instructions>`<br>`    RETURN (expression)`<br>`}`<br><br>Block:<br>`PROCEDURE name  parameter1,`<br>`                parameter2,...`<br>`    instructions`<br>`    RETURN expression` | A procedure, `name`, takes zero or more parameters. The procedure contains programming instructions and returns the value of `expression`. The `RETURN` statement may appear at any point inside the procedure and causes an immediate return from the procedure back to the calling program. |

| Instruction | Explanation |
|---|---|
| **Robot** ||
| If the robot attempts to move to a square that is not open or is beyond the edge of the grid, the robot will stay in its current location and the program will terminate. ||
| Text:<br>`MOVE_FORWARD ()`<br><br>Block:<br>`MOVE_FORWARD` | The robot moves one square forward in the direction it is facing. |
| Text:<br>`ROTATE_LEFT ()`<br><br>Block:<br>`ROTATE_LEFT` | The robot rotates in place 90 degrees counterclockwise (i.e., makes an in-place left turn). |
| Text:<br>`ROTATE_RIGHT ()`<br><br>Block:<br>`ROTATE_RIGHT` | The robot rotates in place 90 degrees clockwise (i.e., makes an in-place right turn). |
| Text:<br>`CAN_MOVE (direction)`<br><br>Block:<br>`CAN_MOVE direction` | Evaluates to `true` if there is an open square one square in the direction relative to where the robot is facing; otherwise evaluates to `false`. The value of direction can be `left`, `right`, `forward`, or `backward`. |